Nurturing Character in the Classroom

Ethical Motivation

EthEx Series Book 3

Nurturing Character in the Classroom, EthEx Series

Ethical Sensitivity
Ethical Judgment
Ethical Motivation
Ethical Action

CURRICULUM & COURSE-BASED TEXTS & RESOURCES DIVISION

Alliance for Catholic Education Press
at the University of Notre Dame

Nurturing Character in the Classroom

Ethical Motivation

EthEx Series Book 3

Darcia Narvaez, Ph.D.
James Lies, C.S.C., Ph.D.

ALLIANCE FOR CATHOLIC EDUCATION PRESS
AT THE UNIVERSITY OF NOTRE DAME

Notre Dame, Indiana

Alliance for Catholic Education Press
at the University of Notre Dame
158 IEI Building
Notre Dame, IN 46556
http://www.nd.edu/~acepress

Text design by Tonia Bock
Cover design by Mary Jo Adams Kocovski

ISBN: 978-0-9819501-2-9

Library of Congress Cataloging-in-Publication Data

Narvaez, Darcia.
Ethical motivation / Darcia Narvaez, James Lies.
p. cm. -- (Nurturing character in the classroom, EthEx series ; bk. 3)
Includes bibliographical references and index.
Summary: "Provides framework and instructional materials for integrating ethical education, specifically ethical motivation, into the middle school classroom and curriculum"--Provided by publisher.
ISBN 978-0-9819501-2-9 (pbk. : alk. paper)
1. Moral education (middle school)--United States. 2. Ethics--Study and teaching (Middle school)--United States. I. Lies, James, 1962- II. Title.

LC268.N2385 2009
372.01'14--dc22

2009005565

This book was printed on acid-free paper.

Printed in the United States of America.

Table of Contents

Foreword

For the past several years my colleagues and I at the University of Minnesota, in partnership with the Minnesota Department of Children, Families and Learning, have been developing a model for character education in the middle grades that we call "Community Voices and Character Education." Here are the six key characteristics of our model.

First, we adopt a skills-based understanding of moral character. This is not a new idea. Plato believed that the just person is like an artisan who has particular, highly-cultivated skills that have been developed through training and practice (Plato, 1987). Persons of good character, then, have better developed skills in four areas: ethical sensitivity, ethical judgment, ethical motivation, and ethical action (Narvaez, Mitchell, Endicott, & Bock, 1999). For example, experts in the skills of Ethical Sensitivity are better at quickly and accurately "reading" a moral situation and determining what role they might play (Narvaez & Endicott, 2009). Experts in the skills of Ethical Judgment have many tools for solving complex moral problems (Narvaez & Bock, 2009). Experts in the skills of Ethical Motivation cultivate an ethical identity that leads them to prioritize ethical goals (Narvaez & Lies, 2009). Experts in the skills of Ethical Action know how to keep their "eye on the prize," enabling them to stay on task and take the necessary steps to get the ethical job done (Narvaez, 2009). Our approach to character development, then, insists on a holistic understanding of the moral person (Narvaez, Bock, & Endicott, 2003). It views character as a set of component skills that can be cultivated to high levels of expertise.

Expertise is a notion that has gained prominence among educational researchers (e.g., Sternberg, 1998, 1999). According to this view, children move along a continuum from novice-to-expert in each content domain that they study. Unlike novices, experts have larger, more complex and better organized knowledge (Chi, Glaser, & Farr, 1988; Sternberg, 1998). Experts see the world differently (Neisser, 1967). Their extensive pattern matching capabilities allow experts to notice things that novices miss (Novick, 1988). Experts possess well-developed sets of procedural skills. Unlike novices, experts know *what* knowledge to access, *which* procedures to apply, *how* to apply them, and *when* it is appropriate (Abernathy & Hamm, 1995; Hogarth, 2001).

Second, to help children develop character skills in the way that experts do, we adopt a scientifically-based, cognitive approach to learning and teaching that assumes that children actively construct representations of the world (Narvaez, 2002; Piaget, 1932/1965, 1952, 1970). Best practice instruction provides opportunities for students to develop more accurate and better organized representations and the procedural skills required to use them (Anderson, 1989). Like the expert, students learn to master the defining features and underlying structures of a domain through practice that is focused, extensive, and coached (Ericsson & Charness, 1994; Ericsson, Krampe, & Tesch-Roemer, 1993). The educator provides authentic learning experiences that are structured according to what we know about levels of apprenticeship (Marshall, 1995; Rogoff, Baker-Sennett, Lacasa, & Goldsmith, 1995).

Third, our model insists that character development be embedded within standards-driven academic instruction, for ultimately this is the only way character education will be sustained.

Fourth, character should be taught across the curriculum in every subject and activity, for character skills are required not in isolation but throughout every encounter in life.

Fifth, our model opens character education to greater accountability, in the sense that skills are teachable and progress toward mastery can be measured.

Sixth, a curricular approach to character education must be an intentional collaboration with "community voices." After all, students are apprentices to the community. The issue of "whose values will be taught?" is best approached by embedding educational goals within the value commitments of particular communities.

Does this model work? Our preliminary data are quite promising. For example, classrooms using our approach showed increases in scores on prosocial responsibility, ethical identity, and prosocial risk-taking, while a comparison group did not.

In summary, moral character is best thought of as a set of teachable, ethically-relevant skills. Ethical skill instruction should be embedded in standards-driven pedagogy. Ethical skills should be taught across the curriculum and cultivated by community voices. With such an education, students will develop schemas of goodness and of justice. They will learn routines of helping and of reasoning. They will learn skills of leadership and of commitment. With these skills they can take responsibility for ethical action in their neighborhoods and in their communities. They will be energized by memories of personal ethical action. With these skills, students are empowered to be active citizens who will make the fate of the nation their own.

Speech at the Whitehouse Conference on Character and Community
Darcia Narvaez, Ph.D.
Associate Professor, University of Notre Dame
June 2002

References

Abernathy, C. M., & Hamm, R. M. (1995). *Surgical intuition.* Philadelphia: Hanley & Belfus.

Anderson, L. M. (1989). Learners and learning. In M. C. Reynolds (Ed.), *Knowledge base for the beginning teacher* (pp. 85-99). Oxford: Pergamon Press.

Chi, M. T. H., Glaser, R., & Farr, M. (1988). *The nature of expertise.* Hillsdale, NJ: Erlbaum.

Ericsson, K. A., & Charness, N. (1994). Expert performance: Its structure and acquisition. *American Psychologist, 49,* 725-747.

Ericsson, K. A., Krampe, R. T., & Tesch-Roemer, C. (1993). The role of deliberate practice in the acquisition of expert performance. *Psychological Review, 100*(3), 363-406.

Hogarth, R. M. (2001). *Educating intuition.* Chicago: University of Chicago Press.

Marshall, S. P. (1995). *Schemas in problem solving.* Cambridge: Cambridge University Press.

Narvaez, D. (2002). Does reading moral stories build character? *Educational Psychology Review, 14*(2), 155-171.

Narvaez, D. (2009). *Ethical action: Nurturing character in the classroom, EthEx Series, Book 4.* Notre Dame, IN: Alliance for Catholic Education Press.

Narvaez, D., & Bock, T. (2009). *Ethical judgment: Nurturing character in the classroom, EthEx Series, Book 2.* Notre Dame, IN: Alliance for Catholic Education Press.

Narvaez, D., Bock, T., & Endicott, L. (2003). Who should I become? Citizenship, goodness, moral flourishing, and ethical expertise. In W. Veugelers & F. Oser (Eds.), *Teaching in moral and democratic education.* Bern: P. Lang.

Narvaez, D., & Endicott, L. (2009). *Ethical sensitivity: Nurturing character in the classroom, EthEx Series, Book 1.* Notre Dame, IN: Alliance for Catholic Education Press.

Narvaez, D., & Lies, J. (2009). *Ethical motivation: Nurturing character in the classroom, EthEx Series, Book 3.* Notre Dame, IN: Alliance for Catholic Education Press.

Narvaez, D., Mitchell, C., Endicott, L., & Bock, T. (1999). *Nurturing character in the middle school classroom: A guidebook for teachers.* St. Paul, MN: Department of Children, Families, and Learning.

Neisser, U. (1967). *Cognitive psychology.* New York: Appletown-Century-Crofts.

Novick, L. R. (1988). Analogical transfer, problem similarity, and expertise. *Journal of Experimental Psychology: Learning, Memory, & Cognition, 14*(3), 510-520.

Piaget, J. (1952). *The origin of intelligence in children.* New York: International University Press.

Piaget, J. (1965). *The moral judgment of the child* (M. Gabain, Trans.). New York: Free Press. (Original work published 1932)

Piaget, J. (1970). *Genetic epistemology* (E. Duckworth, Trans.). New York: Columbia University Press.

Plato. (1987). *The republic.* London: Penguin.

Rogoff, B., Baker-Sennett, J., Lacasa, P., & Goldsmith, D. (1995). Development through participation in sociocultural activity. *Cultural Practices as Contexts for Development: New Directions for Child and Adolescent Development, 67,* 45-64.

Sternberg, R. (1998). Abilities are forms of developing expertise. *Educational Researcher, 3,* 22-35.

Sternberg, R. (1999). Intelligence as developing expertise. *Contemporary Educational Psychology, 24*(4), 359-375.

Preface

The *Nurturing Character in the Classroom, EthEx Series* materials were developed under the auspices of the Minnesota Community Voices and Character Education project (grant# R215V980001 from the U. S. Department of Education Office of Educational Research and Improvement to the Minnesota Department of Children, Families and Learning during 1998-2002).

The *Nurturing Character in the Classroom, EthEx Series* materials were developed in collaboration with teachers across the state of Minnesota and were tested throughout the project by volunteer teams of educators. **For a report of the final-year evaluation, see Narvaez, Bock, Endicott, and Lies (2004).**

EthEx refers to the lifelong development of ethical skills toward expertise (**eth**ical **ex**pertise) in many domains and situations. The four EthEx books (sensitivity, judgment, motivation, action) suggest skills and subskills required for virtuous life. The books also lay out how to teach them through four levels of expertise development.

EthEx is incorporated into the **Integrative Ethical Education** model (Narvaez, 2006, 2007, 2008, in press). The Integrative Ethical Education model has five steps for educators including (along with EthEx) the importance of a caring relationship with each student, a supportive climate (for achievement and character), student self-regulation for character and achievement, and restoring community networks and support.

These booklets were developed for the middle school level (ages 11-15), but elementary and high school teachers have used them successfully as well.

For **staff development** in your school, please contact Darcia Narvaez at the University of Notre Dame, Department of Psychology (dnarvaez@nd.edu). For questions or other materials, also contact Dr. Narvaez.

References

Narvaez, D. (2006). Integrative ethical education. In M. Killen & J. Smetana (Eds.), *Handbook of moral development* (pp. 703-733). Mahwah, NJ: Erlbaum.

Narvaez, D. (2007). How cognitive and neurobiological sciences inform values education for creatures like us. In D. Aspin & J. Chapman (Eds.), *Values education and lifelong learning: Philosophy, policy, practices* (pp. 127-159). Dordrecht, The Netherlands: Springer Press International.

Narvaez, D. (2008). Human flourishing and moral development: Cognitive science and neurobiological perspectives on virtue development. In L. Nucci & D. Narvaez (Eds.), *Handbook of moral and character education* (pp. 310-327). New York: Routledge.

Narvaez, D. (in press). *Moral development: A pragmatic approach to fostering engagement and imagination.*

Narvaez, D., Bock, T., Endicott, L., & Lies, J. (2004). Minnesota's voices and character education project. *Journal of Research in Character Education, 2,* 89-112.

Acknowledgments

Thanks to former University of Minnesota Team Members and affiliates whose ideas or efforts were influential at one point or another in the development of materials: Christyan Mitchell, Jolynn Gardner, Ruth Schiller, and Laura Staples.

Thanks to Connie Anderson, Minnesota Department of Children, Families and Learning, for her wisdom and leadership throughout the Community Voices and Character Education Project.

Special thanks to our school-based collaborators from across the state of Minnesota who kept us focused on what really works and what really helps the classroom teacher.

Introduction to the Ethical Expertise Model (EthEx)

Purpose and Goals of the EthEx Model

At the beginning of the 21st century, children are less likely to spend time under adult supervision than they were in the past. As a result, children's ethical education has become haphazard, and subject to strong influence from popular media. To help the development of children, we seek to assist educators develop curricula that teach character while simultaneously meeting regular academic requirements. We apply research-based theory to instruction for ethical development, using an expertise model of ethical behavior that is based on research and applied to ethics education.

The Four Guide Books for Teachers

We have created four books[1] that address the four main psychological processes involved in behaving ethically: Ethical Sensitivity, Ethical Judgment, Ethical Motivation, and Ethical Action. Each book provides suggestions for ways to work on the skills of the process within regular lessons. Each book links ethics education to regular academic requirements. The four books are designed to help teachers develop a conscious and conscientious approach to helping students build character.

Why Not a Curriculum?

There are several problems with set curricula. First, the lessons are written out of the context of the classroom for which they are designed to be used. Consequently, no pre-fabricated lesson is actually taught exactly as designed because the teacher must adapt it to the students and class at hand. Second, we have seen too many curricula used once or twice and set aside as other demands claim teacher attention. So, although a set curriculum may appear more useful to the teacher at the outset, in the end it can become "old" as the latest mandate takes precedence. Third, an outside, packaged curriculum is often not assimilated into the teacher's way of thinking about instruction. Hence, it may feel "alien" to the teacher, a feeling that is correspondingly felt by students. So we believe that the best way to change teaching over the long term is to help teachers modify what they already teach. We make suggestions for changes, but the teacher herself modifies lessons in ways that work for her and her students. We believe that teacher tailoring is an approach that can bring lasting change.

[1]These materials have been developed under the auspices of grant # R215V980001 from the U.S. Department of Education Office of Educational Research and Improvement.

Should Teachers Teach Values?
They already are

To educate a person in mind and not in morals is to educate a menace to society.
-Theodore Roosevelt

The United States at the beginning of the 21st century has reached a new pinnacle. There is more prosperity throughout the society than ever before. There are more equal rights across groups (e.g., males and females, minorities and majorities) than at any time in the history of the world. There are comforts U.S. citizens enjoy that are accessible only to the wealthy in many other nations of the world (e.g., clean water, sewage, inexpensive clothes, and food). Then why are children around the nation shooting their peers at school? Why do so many lament our public behavior and sense of community? Why do some argue that our social supports are the worst among industrialized countries of the world (e.g., no national day care, few national benefits for parents)? Why does the U.S. have a greater percentage of its citizens imprisoned than any other nation save Russia? Certainly there are multiple causes for these outcomes. Many people, however, are concerned about the cultural health of our nation.

What do you think of our nation's cultural health? Take, for example, current standards for public behavior—are they better or worse than in the past? What do you think of popular culture? Television shows use language, discuss topics, and show interactions that would not have been broached just a few years ago. For the sake of entertainment, committed couples allow themselves to be placed on "Temptation Island" in order to test how committed they really are. Is that all right? On the popular show "The Ozbournes" the parents fully use profanity. Does it matter? Professional athletes can be felons and still receive acclaim from fans and the news media. Should we care? Many have noted that citizens are increasingly impatient, self-absorbed, and rude in public. Have you noticed? Most notably, people are harming and killing others over traffic offenses (e.g., Road Rage Summit, Minneapolis, April 29, 1999).

Citizens of other industrialized nations are appalled by our culture and consider us a nation of self-indulgent adolescents:

> Americans are like children: noisy, curious, unable to keep a secret, not given to subtlety, and prone to misbehave in public. Once one accepts the American's basically adolescent nature, the rest of their culture falls into place and what at first seemed thoughtless and silly appears charming and energetic. (Faul, 1994, p. 5)

Do you agree? Do you believe that individuals in the United States overemphasize their rights with little thought for their responsibilities to others? Do they (we) overemphasize individualism at the expense of collective goals as communitarians contend (e.g., Bellah, Madsen, Sullivan, Swidler, & Tipton, 1985; Etzioni, 1994)? According to this perspective, everyone is rushing from one activity to another with little thought for neighbors. The patience that is learned from long-time interaction with neighbors is not being fostered. Instead, impatience with others seems the norm. Miss Manners concurs, believing that we have a civility crisis.

Consider today's families. At the dawn of the 21st century in the United States, it is normal for parents (supported by corresponding laws and social beliefs) to think of themselves as individuals first and family members second, making it easy to divorce a spouse even when there are children. Even as a single parent works hard to support the family (or both parents work to maintain a standard of living formerly supported by one income), many are unable to provide the support and supervision their children need (Steinberg, 1996). As a result, children are not getting enough adult attention. A third of them are depressed. Too many commit suicide. They turn to their peers for values, support, and goals.[2] Children spend more time with television, with all its contemporary crudities, than with their parents. Children's values are cultivated willy-nilly by their daily experience largely apart from adults. Some young people admire Eminem, a White rap singer whose songs are replete with the raping or killing of women (including his mother). In fact, some sociologists and philosophers have suggested that U.S. culture, in its fascination with killing, is a culture not only of violence but of death. Such are the values that children bring to school.

"So what?" you might say. "I try not to make judgments about the cultures of my students. I let the students make up their own minds. I don't teach values in my classroom." Really? Is any behavior acceptable in your room? If not, you are teaching values; you are indicating that some behaviors are better than others. Not hitting is better than hitting. Not cheating is better than cheating. On a daily basis, you decide which students or behaviors get rewarded and which get punished. Teachers make decisions about how "the benefits and burdens of living together are distributed" (Rest, 1986). Teachers decide how to manage the competition and cooperation that humans bring to social interactions. In short, teachers are teaching values all day long.

[2] Unlike most other industrialized nations, there are few social supports outside the home that are built into our system; it was designed to rely on the strength of the nuclear family and extended family. A high rate of single parenting, both parents working and the resultant guilt, lack of parenting skills, lack of extended family support, and a cultural milieu oriented to pleasure rather than self-sacrifice all contribute to the decline in communal satisfaction. Instead of child raising being shared across society, the schools are shouldering the many needs that growing (and neglected or abused) children have.

Teachers' Ethical Decisions

We urge teachers to be both conscious of and conscientious about the values they are teaching.

There are many morally-relevant situations in schools in which teachers make decisions that affect student welfare. Here are a few concrete examples of value teaching:

- When teachers **divide the class into groups**, they are conveying what should be noticed (e.g., gender) and what they value (e.g., cooperation, achievement). By doing this they reinforce what students should notice and value.
- When teachers **discipline** students, the students learn what behaviors are important in that classroom (or in the hallway, depending on where the disciplining takes place).
- The **school rules the teacher enforces (or doesn't enforce)** reveal how seriously the students should take rules in school and in general.
- The **standards a teacher applies** to behavior, homework, and attitudes are practiced (and learned) by the students in the classroom.
- **The way a classroom is structured physically** and the way the teacher sets up procedures (and which ones) demonstrate the values held by the teacher. For example, if the teacher wants to emphasize creativity he or she may have colorful decor, alternating seating arrangements, and may allow freedom of choice in selecting academic activities.
- **The teacher's communication style** (quiet and firm, or playful and easy going) can set the climate and convey expectations for behavior.
- Whether or not and how teachers **communicate with parents** show how parents are valued.
- **Grading policies** are another way that teachers distribute the benefits and burdens available in the classroom—does the teacher use norm-references or criterion-references or contract-based grading?
- **Curriculum content selection** can convey a high regard for one culture over another, one viewpoint over another. Whether or not teachers assign homework over religious holidays (and whose holidays) reveal the teacher's expectations and values.
- **The teacher's cultural assumptions** about the social context and his or her instinctive responses to students convey non-verbally who is valued and who is not. This may be one of the most important features of a classroom for a minority student whose success may be at risk.

In short, teachers teach values whether or not they realize it. We urge teachers to be both conscious and conscientious about the values they are teaching. Hence this book has goals for teacher development. As teachers develop curricula using our principles, they will learn the principles to use in their professional behavior. First, we will discuss the process of ethical behavior. Then we will discuss how to apply this knowledge in the classroom—for both curriculum and for general climate in the classroom. Based on these materials, teachers will be able to design activities and a classroom that promote ethical behavior.

This is not to say that teachers currently are without guidance as to promoting an ethical classroom. Teachers have a code of ethics to which they subscribe when obtaining a license and a position. Notice the table from the National Education Association's Code of Ethics. These codes affect much of what teachers decide and do. Notice that the NEA code is not one of "doing no harm," but is proactive, that is, "doing good."

FROM THE CODE OF ETHICS OF THE EDUCATION PROFESSION

(National Education Association, 1975)

Principle 1: Commitment to the student.

In fulfillment to the student, the educator

1. Shall not unreasonably restrain the student from independent action in the pursuit of learning.
2. Shall not unreasonably deny the student access to varying points of view.
3. Shall not deliberately suppress or distort subject matter relevant to the student's progress.
4. Shall make reasonable effort to protect the student from conditions harmful to learning or to health and safety.
5. Shall not intentionally expose the student to embarrassment or disparagement.
6. Shall not on the basis of race, color, creed, sex, national origin, marital status, political or religious beliefs, family, social or cultural background, or sexual orientation, unfairly:
    a. Exclude any student from participation in any program;
    b. Deny benefits to any student;
    c. Grant any advantage to any student.

The NEA code requires teachers:

* to present more than one viewpoint,
* to present the full gamut of subject matter relevant to the student,
* to protect the student from harm.

These are actions that require conscious deliberation. For example, questions the teacher might consider are: What are multiple viewpoints on this topic? What content should be included? What harms students and how can I design an environment and classroom atmosphere that is least harmful? What if a student has a viewpoint that is legitimately harmful or wrong? If the teacher does not deliberately plan around these issues, chances are there will be only mainstream viewpoints presented, the subject matter will be narrow, and the student may have to tolerate insults and other harm from peers.

We believe that there is more to ethical education than even following a code of ethics. The code provides a minimal set of general guidelines. Promoting ethical behavior in students requires not only a deliberate effort but a theory for what ethical behavior entails. In character education programs across the country, it is not always clear what direction these efforts should take. That is the topic of the next section.

What Should Be Taught?
The Process Model of Ethical Behavior

When a curriculum claims to be educating for character, what should it mean? What are the aspects of ethics that should be addressed? As a framework for analysis, we use the process model of ethical behavior as described by Rest (1983) and advocated by Bebeau, Rest, and Narvaez (1999). The model includes ethical sensitivity, ethical judgment, ethical motivation, and ethical action. See the framework outlined below and described in the next section.

The Process Model of Ethical Behavior

ETHICAL SENSITIVITY

NOTICE!

Pick up on the cues related to ethical decision making and behavior; Interpret the situation according to who is involved, what actions to take, and what possible reactions and outcomes might ensue.

ETHICAL JUDGMENT

THINK!

Reason about the possible actions in the situation and judge which action is most ethical.

ETHICAL MOTIVATION

AIM!

Prioritize the ethical action over other goals and needs (either in the particular situation, or as a habit).

ETHICAL ACTION

ACT!

Implement the ethical action by knowing how to do so and follow through despite hardship

How the Ethical Process Model Works

A kindergarten student in New York City dies midyear from longstanding child abuse at the hands of a parent. The community is shocked that the teacher and school did not prevent the untimely death.

The star of the boy's basketball team is flunking English. If he gets a failing grade, he won't be able to play on the team. Should the teacher give him a passing grade so that the team has a chance to win the championship and boost school morale?

An American Indian student won't look the teacher in the eye nor volunteer answers in class. How should the teacher respond?

From large effects to small, the ethical behavior of teachers—or the lack thereof—influences children's lives on a daily basis (e.g., Bergem, 1990; Goodlad, Soder, & Sirotnik, 1990). Decisions about grading and grouping; decisions about curriculum, instructional style, assessment; decisions about the allotment of time, care, and encouragement (which students, when, where, and how?)—all of these are ethical decisions the educator faces each day. How can teachers sort out the processes of ethical decision making?

First, one must know what ethical behavior looks like. When thinking about ethical behavior, it is often helpful to think of ethical failure. For example, albeit an extreme one, think of the teacher whose student dies from child abuse. How is it that the teacher did not take ethical action and intervene? There are many points at which failure might have occurred. First, the teacher would have to recognize the signs and symptoms of abuse, and have some empathic reaction to the child's circumstance. Having noticed and felt concern, the teacher would need to think about what action might be taken and what outcomes might occur. Then the teacher must reason about the choices and decide which action to take. (In order for ethical behavior to eventually occur, the teacher would need to select an ethical action). Next, the teacher would need to prioritize the chosen (ethical) action over other needs, motives, and goals. Finally, the teacher would need to know what steps to take to implement the decision, and persevere until the action was completed. It is apparent that there are a lot of places where things can go wrong. For example, the teacher may not see the signs or may make a bad judgment or may have other priorities or may not know what to do or may give up in frustration. In effect, ethical failure can stem from any one or more of these weaknesses.

Rest (1983) has asked: What psychological elements are involved in bringing about an ethical action? He has suggested that there are at least four psychological processes of ethical behavior that must occur in order for an ethical behavior to ensue. These four processes are:

(1) *Ethical Sensitivity:* Noticing the cues that indicate a moral situation is at hand. Identifying the persons who are interested in possible actions and outcomes and how the interested parties might respond to the range of possible actions and outcomes.

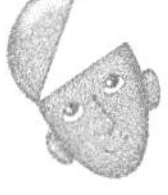

(2) *Ethical Judgment:* Making a decision about what is ethically right or ethically wrong in the situation.

(3) *Ethical Motivation:* Placing the ethical action choice at the top of one's priorities, over all other personal values at the moment.

(4) *Ethical Action:* Having the necessary ego strength and implementation skills to complete the action despite obstacles, opposition, and fatigue.

In an effort to make these processes clear, let us look at a specific situation in a classroom to which we will apply the processes. Let us imagine that Mr. Anderson has a classroom of children in which Abraham is hitting Maria. Now let us look at each of the processes in relation to this event.

Process 1: Ethical Sensitivity

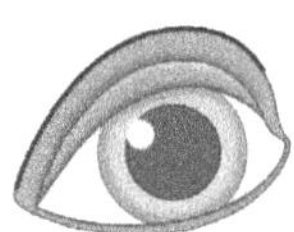

Picking up on the cues related to ethical decision making and ethical behavior. Interpreting the situation according to who is involved, what actions to take, what possible reactions and outcomes might ensue.

Teachers need to be able to detect and interpret environmental cues correctly in order for the other processes of ethical behavior to be initiated. For example, if Mr. Anderson completely fails to see Abraham hitting Maria, there will be no consideration of action choices or action taken. In order to perceive the action, such an occurrence must be salient because, for example, it is unusual. On the other hand, Mr. Anderson may not notice the hitting if it is a daily class-wide event, or if it is an agreed-upon sign of affection.

Ethical Sensitivity

Notice a problem (sensibilities)
What kinds of problems are salient to me, my family, my community, my affiliative groups?

State the situation (critical thinking)
What is the problem? How did the problem come about? How much time is there to make a decision? How does my community identify the problem? How do elders in my family identify the problem? How does my religion or family culture affect my perceptions?

State the interested parties (critical thinking)
Who are the people who will be affected by this decision (family, community, affiliative groups)? Who should be consulted in this decision? Who has faced this problem before? With whom could I talk about the problem?

Weigh the possible outcomes—short-term and long-term (creative thinking)
What are the possible consequences to me, my family/community/affiliative groups for each possible action? What are the possible reactions of these interested parties? What are the potential benefits for me, my family/community/affinity groups for each possible action? Who else might be affected? How will my choice affect the rest of the world now and in the future?

List all possible options (creative thinking)
How could the problem be solved? What are the choices I have for solving the problem? How would my community/family/cultural group solve the problem? What are the choices my family/cultural/community allow? Should I consider other options?

In intercultural/intersocial-class situations, cue misperception may take place, leading to improper action or no action at all. For example, a middle-class teacher in the U.S.A. may subconsciously perceive the downcast eyes of a Native American student in conversation with her as a sign of disrespect toward her authority. But in the student's own culture, the opposite is the case. However, out of ignorance the teacher may take an action to re-establish her authority, for example, punish the child. In contrast, a child may exhibit disrespectful behavior for his own subculture, such as severe slouching for some African-American communities.

However, this action is not really noticed since it is not considered out of the ordinary by the non-African-American teacher or interpreted as a threat to her authority (which it is intended to be) but is considered to be an acceptable expression of frustration on behalf of the student. In this case, the teacher interprets (subconsciously) the child's behavior as a personal freedom issue rather than the challenge to authority (a responsibility issue) that it is.

Ethical sensitivity includes subconscious processing which is often culturally based. As such, teachers need to become aware of their culturally-based expectations and to broaden their understanding of other cultural perspectives in order to circumvent misinterpretation of student behavior.

Not only is Mr. Anderson faced with many perceptual cues to sort through each day, he is also faced with countless situations in which he must make decisions with partial information. Before making a decision, he must interpret situations contextually, according to who is interested in the outcome, what actions and outcomes are possible and how the interested people might react to each. Many problems are much more complicated than in our example (e.g., whether or not to promote a student to the next grade). Here, it is obvious that hitting is generally wrong.

In our incident with Abraham and Maria, Mr. Anderson has noticed the action and finds it out of the ordinary and unacceptable. Now he must determine who is interested in the decision he makes about the incident—certainly Abraham and Maria would be interested, as well as their parents and families, the school administrator, not to speak of the other children in the classroom. Next, he thinks about the actions he could take in this situation and the likely outcomes and reactions of interested parties. For example, he might quickly think:

> *Well, I could stop what I am doing and verbally intervene in front of the whole class. Maybe that is not such a good idea because it would disrupt everyone's work. If Abraham does not stop, other children might notice and perhaps think that hitting was permissible. I could walk over there and physically intervene—grab Abraham's hand. That would stop it and still draw attention from the others—maybe they would learn something. Or, I could ignore it, since Abraham tends to do this when he gets excited—he means no harm. But how would Maria react to that? If I don't do something, Maria's parents might complain to the administrator.*

Ethical sensitivity involves attending to relevant events and mapping out possible actions and their effects. It includes a subtle interaction between both conscious and subconscious processing.

ETHICAL SENSITIVITY SKILLS
ES-1: Understanding Emotional Expression
ES-2: Taking the Perspective of Others
ES-3: Connecting to Others
ES-4: Responding to Diversity
ES-5: Controlling Social Bias
ES-6: Interpreting Situations
ES-7: Communicating Well

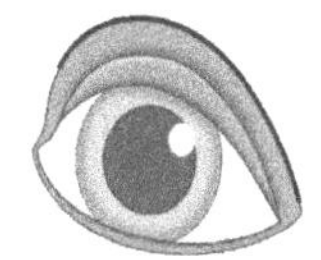

Process 2: Ethical Judgment

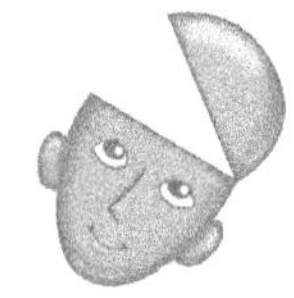

Reasoning about the possible actions in the situation and judging which action is most ethical.

Following this exploration of possible actions and reactions, the ethical actor must decide on which course of action to take. Ethical judgment is the process of making a decision about which action of all the options is the most moral action. Lawrence Kohlberg (1984) defined different ways that people make decisions about how to get along with others (see the chart on p. 15). Whereas in ethical sensitivity, cultural differences are particularly important, in moral judgment, normative developmental trends in moral judgment are important. The types of moral reasoning Kohlberg found are developmental and have been identified in dozens of countries around the world. Although there are other types of criteria individuals use to make ethical decisions, Kohlberg's framework has extensive empirical research support. In addition, the vast majority of research shows no gender differences.

Ethical Judgment

Make a decision
What is the best action to take? What choice should I make? Why?

Ethical judgment concerns choosing the ethical action from the choices considered in the process of ethical sensitivity; this decision will be influenced by the ethical reasoning structures of the decision maker. In other words, Mr. Anderson selects the action that is the most ethical in the particular situation according to his level of ethical judgment development. In our scenario, Mr. Anderson may decide that, out of the choices we listed above, going over to Abraham and physically intervening is the most defensible ethical action:

> *It prevents further harm to Maria, and has ramifications for future behavior by Abraham and the rest of the class. It sends a clear signal both to Abraham and the rest of the class about how the students should NOT treat each other. I can use it as an opportunity to discuss the importance of following rules to keep order and safety in the classroom.*

ETHICAL JUDGMENT SKILLS
EJ-1: Reasoning Generally
EJ-2: Reasoning Ethically
EJ-3: Understanding Ethical Problems
EJ-4: Using Codes and Identifying Judgment Criteria
EJ-5: Understanding Consequences
EJ-6: Reflecting on the Process and Outcome
EJ-7: Coping

SIX CONCEPTUAL STAGES ABOUT COOPERATION AND THEIR CHARACTERISTICS

(From Rest, 1979)

PRECONVENTIONAL LEVEL

Stage 1: The ethicality of obedience: Do what you are told.
- Right and wrong are defined simply in terms of obedience to fixed rules.
- Punishment inevitably follows disobedience, and anyone who is punished must have been bad.

Example: Follow class rules to avoid detention.

Stage 2: The ethicality of instrumental egoism: Let's make a deal.
- An act is right if it serves an individual's desires and interests.
- One should obey the law only if it is prudent to do so.
- Cooperative interaction is based on simple exchange.

Example: Do chores to get allowance.

CONVENTIONAL LEVEL

Stage 3: The ethicality of interpersonal concordance: Be considerate, nice and kind, and you'll make friends.
- An act is good if it is based on a prosocial motive.
- Being ethical implies concern for the other's approval.

Example: Share your gum with the class and people will find you likeable.

Stage 4: The ethicality of law and duty to the social order: Everyone in society is obligated to and protected by the law.
- Right is defined by categorical rules, binding on all, that fix shared expectations, thereby providing a basis for social order.
- Values are derived from and subordinated to the social order and maintenance of law.
- Respect for delegated authority is part of one's obligations to society.

Example: Obey traffic lights because it's the law.

POSTCONVENTIONAL

Stage 5: The ethicality of consensus-building procedures: You are obligated by the arrangements that are agreed to by due process procedures.
- Ethical obligation derives from voluntary commitments of society's members to cooperate.
- Procedures exist for selecting laws that maximize welfare as discerned in the majority will.
- Basic rights are preconditions to social obligations.

Example: Obey traffic lights because they are designed to keep us all safe.

Stage 6: The ethicality of non-arbitrary social cooperation: How rational and impartial people would organize cooperation defines ethicality.
- Ethical judgments are ultimately justified by principles of ideal cooperation.
- Individuals each have an equal claim to benefit from the governing principles of cooperation.

Example: Everyone agrees that traffic lights keep us safe and so they will obey them for the common good.

Process 3: Ethical Motivation

Prioritizing the ethical action over other goals and needs (either in the particular situation, or as a habit).

Following Mr. Anderson's decision about which action is most ethical, he must be motivated to prioritize that action, that is, be ethically motivated. Ethical motivation can be viewed in two ways, as situation-specific and as situation-general. Situation-general motivation concerns the day-to-day attitudes about getting along with others. It is a positive attitude towards ethical action that one maintains day to day. Blasi (1984) and Damon (1984) argue that self-concept has a great deal to do with ethical motivation generally, including attending to professional ethical codes. For instance, if one has a concept that one is an ethical person, one is more likely to prioritize ethical behaviors. Situation-specific ethical motivation concerns the prioritization of the ethical action choice in a particular situation. If all goes well, matching one's professional and personal priorities with possible actions results in ethical motivation, prioritizing the ethical action.

Ethical Motivation

Value identification
What are the values of my family/religion/culture/community? How should these values influence what is decided? How does each possible option fit with these values?

Prioritize the action
Am I willing to forego the benefits of NOT taking this best action?

Ethical motivation means that the person has placed the ethical course of action—which was selected in the process of ethical judgment— at the top of the list of action priorities. In other words, all other competing actions, values and concerns are set aside so that the ethical action can be completed. In other words, does a teacher put aside another priority at the moment, such as taking a break, in order to take an ethical action, such as stopping one student from insulting another? In our situation with Mr. Anderson, in order to continue along the route to completing an ethical action, he would have to put aside any other priority (such as teaching the lesson) and focus on performing the ethical action.

ETHICAL MOTIVATION SKILLS
EM-1: Respecting Others
EM-2: Cultivating Conscience
EM-3: Acting Responsibly
EM-4: Being a Community Member
EM-5: Finding Meaning in Life
EM-6: Valuing Traditions and Institutions
EM-7: Developing Ethical Identity and Integrity

Process 4: Ethical Action

Implementing the ethical action by knowing how to do so and following through despite hardship.

Once Mr. Anderson has determined his priorities, he must complete the action and this requires ethical action. Ethical action involves two aspects: ego strength, the ability to persevere despite obstacles and opposition, and implementation skills, knowing what steps to take in order to complete the ethical action.

Ethical Action

Judge the feasibility of the chosen option
What is my attitude about taking this action? Do I believe it is possible for me to take this action? Do I believe that it is likely I will succeed?

Take action
What steps need to be taken to complete the action? Whose help do I need in my family/community/affiliative group? What back up plan do I have if this doesn't work?

Follow through
How do I help myself follow through on this action? How can others help me follow through? How do I resist giving up? How do I muster the courage to do it?

Reflect
What were the consequences of my decision? How did the decision affect me/my family/community/affiliative groups? Did the results turn out as I planned? In the future, should I change the decision or the decision process?

In our situation, Mr. Anderson might be very tired and have to draw up his strength and energize himself in order to take action. The implementation skills required in our scenario might include the manner of Mr. Anderson's intervention (e.g., severe and degrading reprimand versus a kind but firm reproach; or a culturally-sensitive approach that saves a student's 'face').

Let us consider another example. Perhaps a teacher knows that one of her students is smoking when he goes to the lavatory and she believes that it is best to stop him. Ethical action means that she has the action or fortitude to complete the ethical course of action. Many obstacles can arise to circumvent taking the ethical action. For example, if the student is 6 1/2 feet tall, she may feel physically threatened by the thought of confronting him and not even try. On the other hand, she may or may not know what steps to take to handle the situation. For example, to overcome fear for personal safety, she could ask another (bigger) teacher to help her or may inform the head of the school.

ETHICAL ACTION SKILLS
EA-1: Resolving Conflicts and Problems
EA-2: Asserting Respectfully
EA-3: Taking Initiative as a Leader
EA-4: Planning to Implement Decisions
EA-5: Cultivating Courage
EA-6: Persevering
EA-7: Working Hard

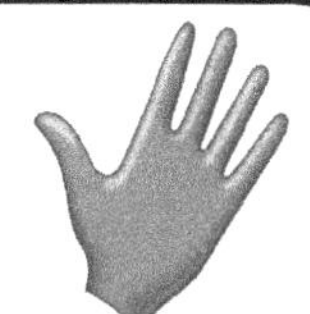

Need for All the Processes

These processes—ethical sensitivity, ethical judgment, ethical motivation, and ethical action—comprise the minimal amount of psychological processing that must occur for an ethical behavior to result. They are highly interdependent. That is, all the processes must be successfully completed before ethical behavior takes place. If one process fails, ethical action will not occur. For instance, if a teacher is highly sensitive to her students and environment but makes poor decisions (e.g., bargaining with students for their cooperation each day), poor outcomes may result. Or, a teacher may be sensitive to the situation, make a responsible ethical judgment, be highly motivated, but lack the backbone to follow through when a student challenges his action.

The processes also interact. That is, one may be so focused on one of the processes that it affects another process. For instance, the teacher who fears for her own safety or who values peace within the classroom may not challenge the students but try to keep them happy by not confronting any miscreant behaviors. Or, a teacher who is extremely tired and wanting to go home to rest may also be less sensitive to the needs of his students and miss cues that indicate ethical conflict.

Teaching Students Ethical Skills

The four-process model outlined here is helpful when thinking about designing instruction to promote ethical behavior. Like teachers, students face ethical dilemmas and situations each day. They have countless opportunities to demonstrate civic and ethical behavior. Their responses may be thoughtful and considerate or may be thoughtless and harmful to self and others. The teacher has a unique opportunity to help students nurture thoughtfulness and consideration of others. Our framework is intended to provide goals for teachers to do so. Our guide booklets suggest methods for reaching these goals during regular instruction.

We parcel each of the four processes into skills. The categorization of skills is not exhaustive but consists of skills that can be taught in a public school classroom. (There are other aspects of the processes that are either controversial or difficult to implement and assess in the public school classroom.) On the next page, we list the whole set of skills that are discussed in the guide booklets.

Ethical Behavior Skills for the Ethical Process Model

Activity Booklet 1: ETHICAL SENSITIVITY

ES-1: Understanding Emotional Expression
ES-2: Taking the Perspective of Others
ES-3: Connecting to Others
ES-4: Responding to Diversity
ES-5: Controlling Social Bias
ES-6: Interpreting Situations
ES-7: Communicating Well

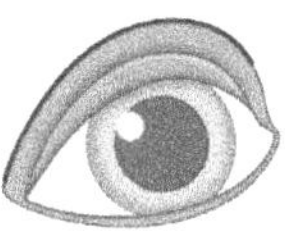

Activity Booklet 2: ETHICAL JUDGMENT

EJ-1: Reasoning Generally
EJ-2: Reasoning Ethically
EJ-3: Understanding Ethical Problems
EJ-4: Using Codes and Identifying Judgment Criteria
EJ-5: Understanding Consequences
EJ-6: Reflecting on the Process and Outcome
EJ-7: Coping

Activity Booklet 3: ETHICAL MOTIVATION

EM-1: Respecting Others
EM-2: Cultivating Conscience
EM-3: Acting Responsibly
EM-4: Being a Community Member
EM-5: Finding Meaning in Life
EM-6: Valuing Traditions and Institutions
EM-7: Developing Ethical Identity and Integrity

Activity Booklet 4: ETHICAL ACTION

EA-1: Resolving Conflicts and Problems
EA-2: Asserting Respectfully
EA-3: Taking Initiative as a Leader
EA-4: Planning to Implement Decisions
EA-5: Cultivating Courage
EA-6: Persevering
EA-7: Working Hard

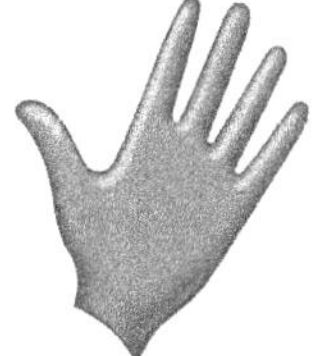

How Should Character Be Taught?
Development Through Levels of Expertise

Each process of the Ethical Expertise Model is divided into several skills. The skills in each process include elements that we think are fundamental and have aspects that can be taught.

We present the skills in terms of expertise development. Think about how a young child learns to talk. First the child is exposed to sounds of all sorts, rather quickly learning the specialness of speech sounds in the environment. The child begins to make sounds, later to mimic and have mock conversations with a responsive caregiver. After many months, an actual word is spoken. From there, the child adds to his or her vocabulary little by little and then in floods. Think of how many hours a child has heard speech before age 2. Think of how much there is to learn yet after age 2. There are many phases of development in language acquisition and mastery. These phases (or levels) are movements toward expertise—toward the eloquence of an Eleanor Roosevelt or William F. Buckley, Jr. We use the notion of expertise in making recommendations for instruction.

Why Use an Expertise Approach?

> Billy has an IQ of 121 on a standardized individual intelligence test; Jimmy has an IQ of 94 on the same test. What do each of these scores, and the difference between them, mean? The ... best available answer to this question is quite different from the one that is conventionally offered—that the scores and the difference between them reflect not some largely inborn, relatively fixed ability construct, but rather a construct of developing expertise. I refer to the expertise that all of these assessments measure as developing rather than as developed because expertise is typically not at an end state but is in a process of continual development. (Sternberg, 1998, p. 11)

Current understanding of knowledge acquisition adopts the construct of novice-to-expert learning. According to this paradigm, individuals build their knowledge over time during the course of experience related to the knowledge domain. Robert Sternberg is a world-renown expert on human abilities and cognition who contends that abilities are developing expertise. Standardized tests measure how much expertise you've developed in a particular subject area or domain (and how much expertise you have at taking such tests).

In general, what do experts have that novices do not have?

Here is a list that Sternberg (1998) garners from research.

- Experts have large, rich, organized networks of concepts (schemas) containing a great deal of declarative knowledge about the domain
- Experts have well-organized, higher interconnected units of knowledge in the domain

What can experts do that novices cannot do?

Sternberg (1998) says that experts can:

- Develop sophisticated representations of domain problems based on structural similarities
- Work forward from given information to implement strategies for finding unknowns in problem solving
- Choose a strategy based on elaborate schemas for problem solving
- Use automated sequences of steps in problem solving
- Demonstrate highly efficient problem solving
- Accurately predict the difficulty of solving certain problems
- Carefully monitor their own problem-solving strategies and process
- Demonstrate high accuracy in reaching appropriate solutions to problems

The level of expertise described by Sternberg requires extensive study and deliberate practice. In primary and secondary schooling, there are many subjects to be covered and little time to spend on each one. Nevertheless, teachers can approach the subject matter as a domain of knowledge that novices can, over time, learn to master. Nurturing mastery of a domain is a lifelong endeavor. Teachers have a chance to help students develop the attitudes and motivation to monitor their own progress toward expertise.

How can novices develop expertise?

Sternberg (1998) suggests that novices should:

- Receive direct instruction to build a knowledge base (lecture, tutoring)
- Engage in actual problem solving
- Engage in role modeling of expert behavior
- Think about problems in the domain and how to solve them
- Receive rewards for successful solution of domain problems

For each skill in a process, we have condensed the complex acquisition of expertise into five skill levels (a larger number would be unmanageable). The purpose of the levels is to give teachers an idea of what students need for developing the given skill, knowledge, or attitude, or what kinds of behavior exhibit a certain level of expertise development. The levels refer to phases of development as both a process (ways to learn a skill) and a product (skills learned). Within each level are many sublevels and supplementary skills that we have not attempted to name. Instead, we use terms that point to the broad processes of building expertise in the domain. The levels are cumulative, that is, each level builds on the previous level. Further, within each skill are many domains. To develop new skills in a domain, the individual circles back through the levels to develop expertise.

Novice-expert differences in the skill categories

Some skill categories are learned from infancy for most people, requiring little conscious effort. For example, *Reading and Expressing Emotion* comes about naturally as a part of learning to get along with others. However, not everyone learns these skills, or learns them well, and few learn them across cultural contexts. Therefore, we include these 'naturally-acquired' skills as areas for all to expand cross-culturally and for some to learn explicitly.

Other skill categories are not learned as a matter of course during childhood. Instead they require concentrated effort. For example, *Controlling Social Bias* does not come naturally to any human or human group. We include these 'studied' skills because they are critical for ethical behavior.

Breaking down the skill category

Although we have parsed the processes into skill categories, the skill categories themselves can be broken down further into sub-skills. We encourage you and your team to do this as much as possible. When you do this, consider what a novice (someone who knows nothing or very little) would need to learn.

On the next page is a brief description of each level of expertise.

Levels of Expertise of an Ethical Behavior Skill

LEVEL 1: IMMERSION IN EXAMPLES AND OPPORTUNITIES

Attend to the big picture, Learn to recognize basic patterns

The teacher plunges students into multiple, engaging activities. Students learn to recognize broad patterns in the domain (identification knowledge). They develop gradual awareness and recognition of elements in the domain.

LEVEL 2: ATTENTION TO FACTS AND SKILLS

Focus on detail and prototypical examples, Build knowledge

The teacher focuses the student's attention on the elemental concepts in the domain in order to build elaboration knowledge. Skills are gradually acquired through motivated, focused attention.

LEVEL 3: PRACTICE PROCEDURES

Set goals, Plan steps of problem solving, Practice skills

The teacher coaches the student and allows the student to try out many skills and ideas throughout the domain to build an understanding of how these relate and how best to solve problems in the domain (planning knowledge). Skills are developed through practice and exploration

LEVEL 4: INTEGRATE KNOWLEDGE AND PROCEDURES

Execute plans, Solve problems

The student finds numerous mentors and/or seeks out information to continue building concepts and skills. There is a gradual systematic integration and application of skills across many situations. The student learns how to take the steps in solving complex domain problems (execution knowledge).

Who Decides Which Values to Teach?
The community

We have presented a set of ethical skills selected according to what enables a person to get along ethically with others and to thrive as a human being. The skills are to be taught developmentally, helping students build expertise. But what do the ethical skills actually look like? For example, what does "respecting others" look like? If one were to travel around the world, the answer would vary. While respect itself is a value worldwide, each community has its own understanding of how it should look. For example, to show respect in some cultures, one speaks quietly and demurely with little eye contact. In other cultures, respect involves looking others in the eye and expressing one's opinions openly. Likewise, "communicating well" or "identifying consequences" can vary across communities. In other words, while in its essence an ethical skill is the same across contexts, it may look different. In the EthEx Model, students learn the different ways a skill appears in their community.

The EthEx Model project emphasizes the importance of embedding the skill categories in community cultural contexts. We encourage communities to be involved in the specific aspects of creating a curriculum for skill development. We hope that the actual day-to-day practice of the skills be determined on site, in the community. Students can gather information about the skill from the community (parents, elders) and bring back that information to the classroom. The teacher can tailor the classroom work to the local understanding of the skill. If there are many interpretations of the skills because of diverse families, this diversity is brought into the classroom by the students themselves.

The goal of any character education program is to build good community members, for it is in communities that students express their values, make ethical decisions, and take ethical action. To be an effective community member in the United States, students need skills for democratic citizenship. These skills are included in the list of ethical skills.

What Is the Student's Role?
To decide his or her own character

The student is not a passive trainee in an EthEx classroom. Through classroom posters and bookmarks, each student is encouraged to think about the following questions: "Who should I be? What should I become?" As teachers approach each skill, these are the questions that should be raised. The teacher can ask students about each skill category, "How do you want to be known?— as [a good communicator, a problem solver, a leader]?" Sometimes the teacher has to identify a particular adult that the student trusts and ask, "What would [so and so] want you to be?" Every day, students should feel empowered with the knowledge that they are creating their own characters with the decisions they make and the actions they take.

The EthEx Model includes both **skills for personal development** and **skills for getting along with others**. All skills are necessary for ethical personhood. The better one knows oneself, the better one can control and guide the self, and the better able one can interact respectfully with others. On the next page we list the skills and the primary focus of each one, which is either on the self or others.

Ethical Behavior Categories for Each Process

The categories are skills the individual needs to develop for reaching individual potential and skills for living a cooperative life with others.

Process Skills	Focus
ETHICAL SENSITIVITY	
ES-1: Understanding Emotional Expression	Self and Others
ES-2: Taking the Perspective of Others	Others
ES-3: Connecting to Others	Others
ES-4: Responding to Diversity	Self and Others
ES-5: Controlling Social Bias	Self
ES-6: Interpreting Situations	Self and Others
ES-7: Communicating Well	Self and Others
ETHICAL JUDGMENT	
EJ-1: Reasoning Generally	Self
EJ-2: Reasoning Ethically	Self
EJ-3: Understanding Ethical Problems	Self and Others
EJ-4: Using Codes and Identifying Judgment Criteria	Self
EJ-5: Understanding Consequences	Self and Others
EJ-6: Reflecting on the Process and Outcome	Self and Others
EJ-7: Coping	Self
ETHICAL MOTIVATION	
EM-1: Respecting Others	Others
EM-2: Cultivating Conscience	Self
EM-3: Acting Responsibly	Self and Others
EM-4: Being a Community Member	Others
EM-5: Finding Meaning in Life	Self and Others
EM-6: Valuing Traditions and Institutions	Self and Others
EM-7: Developing Ethical Identity and Integrity	Self
ETHICAL ACTION	
EA-1: Resolving Conflicts and Problems	Self and Others
EA-2: Asserting Respectfully	Self and Others
EA-3: Taking Initiative as a Leader	Self and Others
EA-4: Planning to Implement Decisions	Self and Others
EA-5: Cultivating Courage	Self and Others
EA-6: Persevering	Self and Others
EA-7: Working Hard	Self

When Should Character Be Taught?
During regular instruction

EthEx stresses the importance of embedding character education into regular, academic, and standards-based instruction. We believe that character education should not stand alone but be incorporated into the entire spectrum of education for students. Regardless of the curriculum, teachers can always raise issues of ethics in lessons.

The second section of this book offers suggestions on how to integrate character development into regular academic instruction. The suggestions in this book are for only one of four processes. We hope you pick up the other three books in order to promote skill development in all processes and skills.

Characteristics of the EthEx Model

Provides a concrete view of ethical behavior
described in *What Should Be Taught?* section (pp. 9-19)

Focuses on novice-to-expert skill building
described in *How Should Character Be Taught?* section (pp. 20-23)

Addresses community cultural contexts
described in *Who Decides Which Values to Teach?* section (p. 24)

Empowers the student
described in *What Is the Student's Role?* section (pp. 25-26)

Embeds character education into regular instruction
described in *When Should Character Be Taught?* section (p. 27)

Ethical Sensitivity

How Ethical Sensitivity Skills Fit with Virtues

SUBSKILL VIRTUE	ES-1 Emotional Expression	ES-2 Taking Persectives	ES-3 Connecting to Others	ES-4 Diversity	ES-5 Controlling Social Bias	ES-6 Interpret Situations	ES-7 Communic-ating Well
Altruism		*	*			*	
Citizenship		*			*	*	*
Civility			*				*
Commitment			*				
Compassion	*	*	*				
Cooperation			*	*	*		*
Courage							
Courtesy			*	*	*		*
Duty							
Fairness		*			*		
Faith			*				
Forbearance	*	*			*		
Foresight		*				*	
Forgiveness					*		
Friendship			*	*			*
Generosity		*	*				
Graciousness	*		*	*		*	*
Hard work							
Helpfulness		*	*			*	
Honesty	*		*				*
Honor							
Hopefulness						*	
Includes others		*	*	*	*	*	*
Justice		*			*		
Kindness	*		*				*
Lawfulness							
Loyalty			*	*			
Obedience							
Obligation							
Patience	*					*	*
Patriotism					*		
Persistence							
Personal Responsibility		*				*	
Politeness	*		*				*
Respect	*		*		*		*
Reverence			*				
Self-control	*						*
Self-sacrifice							
Social Responsibility		*		*	*	*	
Tolerance	*	*		*	*		
Trustworthiness			*				
Unselfishness		*					

Ethical Judgment

How Ethical Judgment Skills Fit with Virtues

VIRTUE / SUBSKILL	EJ-1 Reasoning Generally	EJ-2 Reasoning Ethically	EJ-3 Understand Problems	EJ-4 Using Codes	EJ-5 Conse-quences	EJ-6 Reflecting	EJ-7 Coping
Altruism		*		*		*	
Citizenship		*	*	*		*	
Civility		*		*		*	
Commitment		*		*	*	*	*
Compassion		*	*	*		*	
Cooperation		*				*	
Courage							
Courtesy		*		*		*	
Duty		*		*		*	
Faith		*		*		*	*
Fairness		*	*	*		*	
Forgiveness				*		*	
Friendship		*		*			
Forbearance		*		*		*	*
Foresight	*	*		*			
Generosity		*		*		*	
Graciousness				*			*
Hard work	*	*					
Helpfulness		*		*		*	
Honor		*		*		*	
Honesty		*		*		*	
Hopefulness							*
Includes others		*		*		*	
Justice		*	*	*		*	
Kindness		*		*		*	
Lawfulness		*	*	*		*	
Loyalty		*		*		*	
Obedience		*		*		*	
Obligation		*	*	*		*	
Patience	*				*		*
Patriotism		*		*		*	
Persistence	*						
Politeness				*			
Respect		*		*		*	*
Reverence		*		*		*	*
Personal Responsibility	*	*	*	*		*	
Social Responsibility		*	*	*	*	*	
Self-control					*		*
Self-sacrifice		*				*	
Tolerance		*		*		*	*
Trustworthiness							*
Unselfishness		*		*		*	

Ethical Motivation

How Ethical Motivation Skills Fit with Virtues

SUBSKILL VIRTUE	EM-1 Respecting Others	EM-2 Cultivating Conscience	EM-3 Acting Responsibly	EM-4 Community Member	EM-5 Finding Meaning	EM-6 Valuing Traditions	EM-7 Ethical Identity
Altruism				*	*		*
Citizenship	*	*	*	*		*	
Civility	*	*					*
Commitment		*	*	*	*	*	*
Compassion	*			*	*		*
Cooperation	*	*	*	*	*	*	
Courage		*		*	*		*
Courtesy	*						
Duty	*	*	*			*	
Faith				*	*		*
Fairness				*		*	
Forgiveness	*				*		
Friendship	*						
Forbearance	*	*		*			
Foresight	*		*		*	*	*
Generosity				*			*
Graciousness	*			*			
Hard work			*	*		*	*
Helpfulness	*		*	*			
Honor		*	*		*	*	*
Honesty	*	*					
Hopefulness	*		*	*	*	*	*
Includes others	*			*		*	
Justice						*	
Kindness	*			*			*
Lawfulness		*	*			*	*
Loyalty		*	*			*	*
Obedience		*					
Obligation		*	*	*			
Patience	*		*	*	*	*	
Patriotism						*	
Persistence			*		*	*	*
Politeness	*			*			
Respect	*	*	*	*	*	*	*
Reverence	*	*	*	*	*	*	
Personal Responsibility	*	*	*			*	*
Social Responsibility	*		*	*		*	*
Self-control	*	*	*	*	*		*
Self-sacrifice		*		*			*
Tolerance	*	*	*	*		*	
Trustworthiness		*		*			*
Unselfishness	*	*	*	*	*		*

Ethical Action

How Ethical Action Skills Fit with Virtues

SUBSKILL VIRTUE	EA-1 Resolving Conflicts	EA-2 Assertive-ness	EA-3 Initiative as Leader	EA-4 Planning	EA-5 Cultivating Courage	EA-6 Persevering	EA-7 Working Hard
Altruism			*		*	*	
Citizenship	*		*	*	*	*	*
Civility	*	*				*	
Commitment	*	*	*	*	*	*	*
Compassion		*	*	*	*		*
Cooperation	*	*	*	*			*
Courage		*	*		*		
Courtesy	*	*					
Duty	*		*	*	*	*	*
Fairness	*				*		
Faith			*	*	*		*
Forbearance	*	*	*		*	*	*
Foresight	*	*	*				*
Forgiveness							
Friendship	*			*			
Generosity			*		*		
Graciousness							
Hard work		*	*	*	*	*	*
Helpfulness			*		*	*	*
Honesty		*	*	*			
Honor	*		*	*	*		*
Hopefulness	*	*	*				
Includes others	*		*	*			
Justice	*			*	*		*
Kindness							
Lawfulness			*	*			*
Loyalty			*	*			*
Obedience							*
Obligation	*		*	*			*
Patience	*	*	*			*	*
Patriotism			*	*	*		
Persistence	*	*	*		*	*	*
Personal Responsibility	*		*		*	*	*
Politeness		*		*			
Respect	*	*	*	*			
Reverence			*	*			
Self-control	*	*	*	*		*	*
Self-sacrifice			*		*	*	
Social Responsibility	*		*		*	*	*
Tolerance	*	*	*				
Trustworthiness		*	*				
Unselfishness	*		*	*	*		

References

Bebeau, M., Rest, J. R., & Narvaez, D. (1999). Beyond the promise: A framework for research in moral education. *Educational Researcher, 28*(4), 18-26.

Bellah, R., Madsen, R., Sullivan, W., Swidler, A., & Tipton, S. (1985). *Habits of the heart: Individualism and commitment in American life*. Berkeley: University of California Press.

Bergem, T. (1990). The teacher as moral agent. *Journal of Ethical Education, 19*(2), 88-100.

Blasi, A. (1984). Moral identity: Its role in moral functioning. In W. M. Kurtines & J. L. Gewirtz (Eds.), *Morality, moral behavior, and moral development* (pp. 128-139). New York: Wiley-Interscience.

Damon, W. (1984). Self-understanding and moral development from childhood to adolescence. In W. M. Kurtines & J. L. Gewirtz (Eds.), *Morality, moral behavior, and moral development* (pp. 109-127). New York: Wiley-Interscience.

Etzioni, A. (1994). *The spirit of community: The reinvention of American society*. New York: Simon & Schuster.

Faul, S. (1994). *Xenophobe's guide to the Americans*. London: Ravette.

Goodlad, J., Soder, R., & Sirotnik, K. (1990). *The moral dimensions of teaching*. San Francisco: Jossey-Bass.

Kohlberg, L. (1984). *The psychology of moral development*. New York: Harper & Row.

National Education Association. (1975). *Code of ethics of the education profession*. Retrieved February 5, 2009, from http://ethics.iit.edu/codes/coe/nat.edu.assoc.1975.html

Rest, J. R. (1979). *Development in judging moral issues*. Minneapolis: University of Minnesota Press.

Rest, J. R. (1983). Morality. In P. Mussen (Series Ed.), J. Flavell & E. Markham, (Volume Eds.), *Manual of child psychology: Vol. 3, Cognitive development* (pp. 556-269). New York: Wiley.

Rest, J. R. (1986). *Moral development: Advances in research and theory*. New York: Praeger.

Steinberg, L. (1996). *Beyond the classroom: Why school reform failed and what parents need to do*. New York: Simon and Schuster.

Sternberg, R. (1998). Abilities are forms of developing expertise. *Educational Researcher, 3*, 22-35.

Nurturing Ethical Motivation

Organization of Ethical Motivation Booklet

Overview Pages
Ethical Action skills and subskills

Skill Sections (7 skill sections in all—the ***"meat"*** of the booklet)
Skill Overview (see sample page below)
Subskills (see sample pages on p. 37)
- Activities
- Assessment hints
- Climate suggestions

Appendix
Guide for Lesson Planning
Linking to the Community Worksheet
Rubric Examples
Special Activities
Resources
Linking EA Skills to Search Institute Assets
References

Skill Overview Page

Skill Title	**Persevering** — Ethical Action 6
WHAT the skill is	WHAT Perseverance enables individuals to complete actions that are important to them and others. Without it, many ethical actions would fail at the sight of the first obstacle or difficulty.
WHY the skill is important	WHY Perseverance is important for the completion of an ethical action. Children can be successfully instructed to 'talk to themselves' about not doing something, and instructed on how to distract themselves from unwanted behavior. A form of self-talk to complete a task can be a useful technique to help one find the ego strength to complete an ethical action—at any age.
SUBSKILLS list	SUBSKILLS OVERVIEW Be steadfast Overcome obstacles Build competence

Side header on sample page: EA-6 Developing Perseverance: Overview

Skill Name: Subskill Name
Side Header

Subskill Activities Page

Skill & Subskill NAME

Expert Example

Subskill Activities by Level of Expertise
(4 levels total, usually spans 2-4 pages per subskill)

Persevering by Building Competence

Expert

Christopher Reeves (who played Superman in the movies) had an equestrian accident that left him a quadriplegic. He could have given up in life and stayed home quietly, but he became a spokesman for those with spinal injuries, traveling to speak about the importance of research in spinal injuries.

Ideas for Developing Skills

Level 1: Immersion in Examples and Opportunities
Attend to the big picture, Learn to recognize basic patterns

Study self-efficacy. Discuss how, for a particular field, small successes give a person confidence to keep trying and try harder things. Find examples in literature, television and movies, or in a particular subject area. ★

Level 2: Attention to Facts and Skills
Focus on detail and prototypical examples, Build knowledge

Self-talk. Find examples of and discuss how to 'cheerlead' for yourself in different situations. What behaviors help you do your best and reach excellence? (1) Students discuss self-talk and behaviors that help one persevere. (2) Students interview older students or adults about general behaviors. (3) Students interview adults in roles they admire or strive for in a particular field. ★

Level 3: Practice Procedures
Set goals, Plan steps of problem solving, Practice skills

Examples of pushing oneself in helping others. Students interview elders about their personal experiences of (1) how they persevered in trying to help others; (2) how they persevered in working towards a goal that helped humanity.

Level 4: Integrate Knowledge and Procedures
Execute Plans, Solve Problems

Self-help. Have students practice ways to coach oneself to reach excellence in ... in mental and physical ...eting tasks without

Assessment Hints

Building competence

Use multiple-choice, true-false, short answer, or essay tests to assess student's knowledge of strategies to push oneself.

Have students write reports, based on observations or interviews, of what they learned about pushing oneself.

EA-6 Developing Perseverance: Building competence

Skill Name: Subskill Name
Side Header

Hints for Assessment

Skill Climate Page

Create a Climate to Persevere

Regularly discuss the importance of finishing a task, as a group or individual.

Regularly point out what would happen if people did not persevere until a job was done (e.g., the highway, a bridge, your house, your car) and how it would affect people around them.

Discuss the importance of persevering in meeting your responsibilities to others.

Sample Student Self Monitoring
Persevering

Be steadfast
I wait to reward myself until I've finished my work.
I don't wait until the last minute to do my work.
I lose control when I am angry. (NOT)
I control my feelings of anger.
I resist my impulses to disobey rules.

What you need to know for success in school

1. That attitudes affect behavior
2. That what you believe/think about affects your behavior
3. That you have some control over your attitudes
4. That learning anything requires commitment (decision to put your energies into a task)

EA-6 Developing Perseverance: Climate

Suggestions for Creating a Climate to Develop Skill

Sample Self-Monitoring Questions for Student

Selections to Post in the Classroom for Developing Skill

Ethical Processes & Skills

with Ethical Motivation Subskills

Activity Booklet 1: ETHICAL SENSITIVITY

ES-1 Understanding Emotional Expression
ES-2 Taking the Perspective of Others
ES-3 Connecting to Others
ES-4 Responding to Diversity
ES-5 Controlling Social Bias
ES-6 Interpreting Situations
ES-7 Communicating Well

Activity Booklet 2: ETHICAL JUDGMENT

EJ-1 Reasoning Generally
EJ-2 Reasoning Ethically
EJ-3 Understanding Ethical Problems
EJ-4 Using Codes and Identifying Judgment Criteria
EJ-5 Understanding Consequences
EJ-6 Reflecting on the Process and Outcome
EJ-7 Coping

Activity Booklet 4: ETHICAL ACTION

EA-1 Resolving Conflicts and Problems
EA-2 Asserting Respectfully
EA-3 Taking Initiative as a Leader
EA-4 Planning to Implement Decisions
EA-5 Cultivating Courage
EA-6 Persevering
EA-7 Working Hard

Activity Booklet 3: ETHICAL MOTIVATION

EM-1 Respecting Others
Be civil and courteous
Be non-violent
Show reverence

EM-2 Cultivating Conscience
Self command
Manage influence and power
Be honorable

EM-3 Acting Responsibly
Meet obligations
Be a good steward
Be a global citizen

EM-4 Being a Community Member
Cooperate
Act thoughtfully
Share resources

EM-5 Finding Meaning in Life
Center yourself
Cultivate commitment
Cultivate wonder

EM-6 Valuing Traditions and Institutions
Identify and value traditions
Understand social structures
Practice democracy

EM-7 Developing Ethical Identity and Integrity
Choose good values
Build your identity
Reach for your potential

Ethical Motivation

Ethical Motivation involves prioritizing ethical action over other goals and needs.
This component is influenced by categories in Ethical Sensitivity.

Outline of Skills

EM-1: RESPECTING OTHERS
Respect for others is a core societal value and stems from the belief that others have rights and each has responsibilities towards others that include courtesy and civility. Respect is an attitude that life has inherent value and should be cherished. This extends to treating others non-coercively and without violence.

EM-2: CULTIVATING CONSCIENCE
Conscience is the driving force behind self command and temperance. A sense of conscience is the sense of discomfort, based on a sense of empathy, that one experiences upon realizing the harm, or potential harm, that one may inflict on others. A person of honor has developed skills to control impulses and manage power.

EM-3: ACTING RESPONSIBLY
Acting responsibly might also be called conscientiousness. It is a desire to uphold all the possible ethical obligations one may have. Conscientiousness involves attending to the details of one's obligations, being a good steward of one's talents and wealth, and acting as a global citizen.

EM-4: BEING A COMMUNITY MEMBER
Being a community member is a concrete way to show ethical motivation and requires skills of cooperation and acting thoughtfully. Ways to help include sharing one's resources and being of service to meet needs in the community.

EM-5: FINDING MEANING IN LIFE
Finding meaning in life can be cultivated through teaching students (1) how to center themselves, (2) how to find and work on commitment to good causes, and (3) how to appreciate aesthetic experiences. Centering is the constant practice of calming inner turmoil, relaxing energy and focusing attention. Commitment means dedicating oneself to something wholeheartedly.

EM-6: VALUING TRADITIONS AND INSTITUTIONS
Valuing traditions and institutions means respecting the laws, practices, and organizations of one's society. Respecting them requires an awareness of traditions and the functions of institutions. Members of democratic societies in democracies are obligated to be active citizens and to know the skills that are required for full participation.

EM-7: DEVELOPING ETHICAL IDENTITY AND INTEGRITY
Ethical identity is the perception one has of oneself as an ethical agent. It involves respecting oneself, as well as a positive identification with an ethical role model in order to create a positive ethical identity. Ethical identity motivates ethical action because the person attempts to match an ethical self-concept or ideal with action. The goal of development is to reach one's potential as an ethical, fully functioning individual in community.

Ethical Motivation

WHAT
Ethical motivation has two aspects. One is concerned about completing a particular ethical action. The other is an ethical orientation to everything one does.

WHY
If one is not driven by an ethical identity generally, one may take actions that harm other persons. Similarly, if one does not have an ethical goal in mind when taking an action, one may act in ways that harm the self or others. Ethical motivation is nurtured when one learns to respect others, act responsibly, and develop a positive identity. As with Ethical Sensitivity and Ethical Judgment, there are many aspects of Ethical Motivation that can be taught.

ROLE OF TEACHER/ADULT
Adults model the skills of ethical motivation when they reveal their ideals, mentors, and rationale for action. Adults nurture ethical motivation when they hold high standards for youth that include respect for others, responsible action, and respect for authority.

TACKLING EXCUSES AND HANGUPS

Sometimes students will resist learning or taking action, giving excuses like the following. We offer suggestions about how to counteract these attitudes.

'Why should I bother about them?' (sense of superiority)
Discuss this as a general human bias that one must consciously control.

'Yup, I was right about those homeless people. They're just lazy.'
Discuss the human tendency to look only for confirming evidence of personal bias. Work on perspective-taking.

'I couldn't help it. I was so mad.'
Discuss or demonstrate the benefits of giving emotions a "cooling down period" and being objective.

'It's not my problem.'
Discuss human relatedness (ES-3) and ethical responsibility (EM-4).

'That looks/tastes/smells weird!'
Work on reducing fear of the unknown and difference. Discuss the realistic risks and benefits of learning about something new.

'It's just a TV show. I know it's not real.'
Discuss the harm of desensitization to violence and objectification of people.

'The consequences are too far in the future to concern me.' (This is especially pertinent to young people's attitudes toward drugs, alcohol.) Bring in guest speakers who had these thoughts/attitudes and then experienced the "far off" consequences. Encourage students to discuss issues with the speaker.

'The possible consequences will never happen to me.' (e.g., getting pregnant, being arrested for vandalism, other crimes) Bring in guest speakers who had these thoughts/attitudes and then experienced the "unrealistic" consequences. Encourage students to discuss issues with the speaker.

"The possible consequences will never happen to him/her/them.'
Bring in guest speakers who had these thoughts/attitudes and then witnessed the "improbable" consequences occurring to another (e.g., killing a friend or stranger by driving drunk). Encourage students to discuss issues with the speaker and ask many questions.

'I have no choice—my friends are making me do this.'
Have students practice assertiveness skills: (1) Describe the situation that is upsetting, without blaming or getting emotional. (2) Tell other person your feelings. (3) Tell other person what you want him/her to change. (4) Tell other person how the change would make you feel.

'It's not my fault—person X is who you should blame!'
Counter with techniques to foster feelings of responsibility/accountability for one's own actions: (1) Discipline with immediate consequences and a given reason. (2) Help parents with discipline plans that include giving reasons to students when disciplined. (3) Discuss related dilemmas with slight variations.

'I can't change this situation so I won't try.'
Counter with inspirational examples of how others make a difference (e.g., Rosa Parks, or a local community member who has made a difference). Discuss how student is more similar than different to this person. Emphasize how the student can make a difference.

TACKLING EXCUSES AND HANGUPS (continued)

'This situation is none of my concern.' (e.g., witnessing a fight or a crime)
Counter with citizenship activities, discussing the importance of concern for others in the community and outside of the community. Discuss the purpose of citizenship and its related responsibilities. Study exemplars of good citizenship.

'There's no time to think of other alternatives!'
Discuss (1) human tendencies to lose control (and do harm) when emotions are high, and (2) the importance of carefully and systematically thinking through a dilemma or problem and decision so others and yourself will not be harmed in the immediate or distant future.

'Why should their well-being be my concern?' (lack of positive regard for life)
Encourage a more positive regard for life and discuss in class people who have a healthy regard for life.

'It's not my responsibility to save the world!' (not seeing the value of human existence)
Counter with a discussion of the interconnectedness of us all and our ethical obligations to each other.

'Why should I help them? Nobody's ever done anything for me!' (pessimistic attitude resulting from negative life experience) Discuss the importance of optimism, and of overcoming obstacles.

'It's their own fault that they're in this mess...not mine.' (lack of empathic understanding of others) Foster a discussion of those who are empathic and how to help another in distress.

'I've got other things planned...I don't have time to help!' (having immediate needs that are in opposition to caring for others) Discuss the importance weighing others' needs against our own, developing courtesy, meeting obligations and showing generosity.

'Being a citizen of the U.S.A. means freedom to do what I want.'
Counter with examination and discussion of various forms of citizenship. Discuss the purpose of citizenship and its related responsibilities.

'This is stuff that adults do.'
Discuss examples of the positive and meaningful impact of young people on the world (e.g., dot-com companies, altruistic group leadership, etc.).

'This is the stuff that people in x-group do.'
Give counter examples to sex-typing, group typing.

'Other people will take care of it.'
Discuss this as a general human bias.

'I don't want to look like a fool in front of my classmates.'
Discuss counter examples of young people being seen as assertive, taking action for others and standing out.

'I'm afraid that my classmates might get back at me.' (This may come up especially if the peers are involved in unethical or illegal activities.) Discuss choices of peers, role models and the consequences.

'I don't like people in that group.'
Discuss the changing nature of group membership and feeling 'outside.'

'I can't do it.'
Discuss this as an obstacle to overcome.

Ethical Motivation

How Ethical Motivation Skills Fit with Virtues

SUBSKILL VIRTUE	EM-1 Respecting Others	EM-2 Cultivating Conscience	EM-3 Acting Responsibly	EM-4 **Community Member**	EM-5 Finding Meaning	EM-6 Valuing Traditions	EM-7 Ethical Identity
Altruism				*	*		*
Citizenship	*	*	*	*		*	
Civility	*	*					*
Commitment		*	*	*	*	*	*
Compassion	*			*	*		*
Cooperation	*	*	*	*	*	*	
Courage		*		*	*		*
Courtesy	*						
Duty	*	*	*			*	
Faith				*	*		*
Fairness				*		*	
Forgiveness	*				*		
Friendship	*						
Forbearance	*	*		*			
Foresight	*		*		*	*	*
Generosity				*			*
Graciousness	*			*			
Hard work			*	*		*	*
Helpfulness	*		*	*			
Honor		*	*		*	*	*
Honesty	*	*					
Hopefulness	*		*	*	*	*	*
Includes others	*			*		*	
Justice						*	
Kindness	*			*			*
Lawfulness		*	*			*	*
Loyalty		*	*			*	*
Obedience		*					
Obligation		*	*	*			
Patience	*		*	*	*	*	
Patriotism						*	
Persistence			*		*	*	*
Politeness	*			*			
Respect	*	*	*	*	*	*	*
Reverence	*	*	*	*	*	*	
Personal Responsibility	*	*	*			*	*
Social Responsibility	*		*	*		*	*
Self-control	*	*	*	*	*		*
Self-sacrifice		*		*			*
Tolerance	*	*	*	*		*	
Trustworthiness		*		*			*
Unselfishness	*	*	*	*	*		*

Ethical Motivation 1

Respecting Others

(Respect others)

WHAT

Respect for others is a core societal value and stems from the belief that others have rights and each has responsibilities towards others that include courtesy and civility. Respect is an attitude that life has inherent value and should be cherished. This extends to treating others non-coercively and without violence.

Being Responsive to Others

Part of showing respect is being responsive to others

For example:

Pay attention to others.

Be aware of others and their needs.

Take action to help others in an acceptable way.

WHY

The good order of any civil society depends on respect. Civility 'is the sum of the many sacrifices we are called to make for the sake of living together' (Carter, 1998). To be a civil citizen, the student must understand and practice the elements of civility including respect for creation, courtesy, and trustworthiness. For example, as a component of being trustworthy, honesty (one of the Search Institute's developmental assets) is a critical skill for civility and respect.

SUBSKILLS OVERVIEW

Be Civil and Courteous
Be Non-violent
Show Reverence

ATTITUDES that Can Get in the Way of Being Responsive to Others

I'm afraid of other people's reactions.

I'm afraid to make a mistake.

People don't like me, so why should I pay attention to them?

If I do that, people will think I'm showing off.

I don't know what to do.

No one cares what I do.

Web Wise

See www.great-ideas.org for non-violent and dynamic peace education information

Lesson plans about peace, war, conflict are available at www.esrnational.org

The Peace Corps' World Wise Schools had resources and ideas for global education: www.peacecorps.gov/wws

Respecting Others by Being Civil & Courteous

"Miss Manners," ***Judith Martin***, has become the spokesperson for good manners, for civility and for courtesy. More than by example, through her books and advice columns, Miss Manners provides guidance to all those seeking to perfect their skills in this regard.

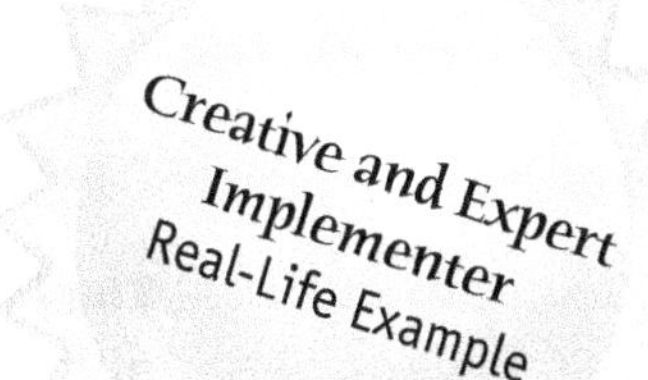

Ideas for Developing Skills

Level 1: Immersion in Examples and Opportunities
Attend to the big picture, Learn to recognize basic patterns

Civility in the classroom. Contrast civil behavior with uncivil behavior, using examples from television (e.g., incivility on the Jerry Springer show). Have students discuss how they would like to be treated—what is civil to them and why? Discuss different ways of being civil, courteous, and mannerly, agreeing on which are necessary in the classroom (e.g., raising one's hand if one has something to say in class). Assess by testing recall of and rationale for the agreed-upon rules.

Good manners as a sign of respect. Read excerpts from a book by Judith Martin (e.g., Martin, 2005). (1) Set up a debate about showing respect through good manners, such as courtesy, politeness, and kindness (for example, premise: "It is important to say 'please' and 'thank you' to show respect"). (2) Have students collect examples of respect and disrespect through the week. Bring all examples back to class and discuss what kinds of actions demonstrate a lack of respect. (3) Have students interview community members/elders about what respect means. Assess by having students write a paragraph about the ways in which they think others should show respect.

> "Civility is liberating. It frees us from slavery to self-absorption, impulse, and mood." (Forni, 2002, p. 22)

Recognizing cruelty. (1) Discuss what cruelty is and what harm there is in being cruel or allowing cruelty. You might use quotes from the rationale that some school shooters have given—which includes being bullied or put down daily (see the website http://www.treas.gov/usss/ntac_ssi.shtml for direct quotes). You might start with a discussion of how people treat animals—sometimes it is easier for people to see the harmful effects on an animal rather than on a human. (2) Discuss the effects of allowing cruelty to continue around you. Find examples of ways to counter cruelty (e.g., do a web search) and have students practice and use the techniques. **Assess** with a knowledge test of how to counter cruelty and/or demonstrations of techniques.

How do you treat a person like a person? (ideas from Pritchard, 1996). Have students discuss each of the following actions according to whether they treat a person as a person. Use these as a source for further discussion. Is it treating a person as person if (a) you keep staring at the person? (b) you yell at the person? (c) you whistle at the person when they walk by? (d) you talk negatively about the person behind their back? (e) you make fun of the person? (f) you listen carefully to what the person has to say? (g) you do everything the person tells you to do? (h) you give the person your lunch money when they ask for it because they are bigger? (i) you throw their books in the garbage? (j) you stop talking to the person when you don't agree with what they say? Ask students to write about how to treat a person as a person.

Starred ★ activities within each subskill go together!

Respecting Others by Being Civil & Courteous

Ideas for Developing Skills

Level 1 (continued)

The importance of being on time. (1) Punctuality as a matter of responsibility. Interview a manager at McDonald's, at a grocery store, or in your neighborhood. Ask the manager how important it is for employees to be on time and how it affects the business if employees are late. Assess by having them write a report about the interview and how what they learned might be applied elsewhere. (2) Punctuality as a matter of civility. (a) Ask students to list school events that they depend on to occur "on time" and conduct a follow-up discussion (e.g., the bell ringing at the end of class, lunch breaks, the school bus arriving as scheduled, and the end of the school year). Ask them how being on time can be an act of courtesy. (b) Discuss cultural differences regarding time. Read about or invite a speaker from a culture where time is viewed as inside oneself, rather than outside oneself in a timepiece (e.g., Native American). Discuss the relation of time to courtesy and civility in this cultural context. (c) Review how being late affects others. Discuss how tardiness to school and class can be a disruption. Stress the fact that late-comers to class miss important information and interrupt the learning in progress. **Assess** by having them write a paragraph about something to which they were late and how it adversely affected others.

Level 2: Attention to Facts and Skills

Focus on detail and prototypical examples, Build knowledge

Respect interviews. Students interview their parents or other adults to find out how they view respect, as well as how they have reacted to instances of disrespect. The following questions may be helpful: What does the word "respect" mean to you? How do you show respect to other people? To be respected, how should a person act? When you were my age, how were you expected to show respect to adults? To authorities? To siblings and friends? Do you feel that adults treated you respectfully when you were my age? Were there any things you wish they had done, or hadn't done? **Assess** with report on interview.

Courtesy in different historical time periods. (1) Students research the rules of courtesy and their relation to citizenship in different time periods (for example, it used to be courteous for women to curtsey and men to take off their hats and bow when meeting). Students can demonstrate what they learned in skits. (2) Discuss the evolution of the rules of courtesy in a particular country or culture. **Assess** by writing reflective essays on a comparison of and their reactions to the different styles.

Starred activities within each subskill go together!

Respecting Others by Being Civil & Courteous
Ideas for Developing Skills

Level 2 (continued)

Describe how tolerance is a sign of civility. Explore the deeper meaning of the word 'tolerance.' Find different definitions, especially those from political scientists. Discuss how tolerance for other people demonstrates and fosters civility. How can we show appreciation for differences in our culture? **Assess** with an essay.

Respecting differences. Discuss the differences that exist among people at school and in the community. Discuss the sources of some of these differences (e.g., genetics/birth, culture, age). Discuss the importance of respect for these differences and what respect looks like. Contrast this with a discussion of behaviors that should not be tolerated or respected, such as violence, the battering of children or spouses, criminal behavior, etc.

Respect yourself. Ask students how they show respect for themselves. (1) What might the way that each of us walks, acts and dresses say about us? (2) Have students interview professionals about how they dress and what they convey in their dress. As a class, discuss the findings from different professions and what is similar/different about their perspectives.

Civility in particular fields. Discuss with students how people demonstrate civility and courtesy to each other in different areas of study (e.g., mathematics, biology) or work (e.g., police work, teaching, professional football). (1) Invite a member of the profession to speak to the class on this topic. (2) Find examples in news and media. (3) Have students interview a professional. (4) Have students conduct research.

How we want to be acknowledged. (1) Throughout the day. (a) Have students list the different individuals and types of people they see throughout the day. (b) Discuss how they would like to be acknowledged by others. (c) For a day or several days, have them practice acknowledging others like they would like to be acknowledged and keep track of how others respond to them. (2) In the classroom. (a) Have the class discuss how they would like to be acknowledged and to acknowledge others within the classroom. (b) Have students practice what they decide for a week or more. (c) Discuss the results of the practices and what to change or keep the same.

Recognizing a subtle "no" (Forni, 2002). Discuss with students the nonverbal ways people say no including: showing reluctance, minimal response, lack of enthusiasm, person paying more attention to something else than to what you want them to do. Discuss the respectful response: Once a person says no, accept it. Don't pester and become annoying, upsetting them with your demands. Then (a) ask students to find examples of the subtle no in a video clip or during class or the school day, or (b) have students give several subtle no's throughout the day and record how people responded.

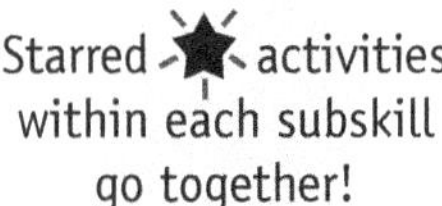
Starred activities within each subskill go together!

Respecting Others by Being Civil & Courteous
Ideas for Developing Skills

Level 3: Practice Procedures
Set goals, Plan steps of problem solving, Practice skills

Respectful encounters. In small groups, students role play several situations such as: (1) new people are meeting for the first time (vary the ages of the people); (2) a stranger asking for help; (3) helping someone who has dropped everything all over the sidewalk; (4) helping someone in a wheelchair who is approaching a door. Students practice courteous acknowledgments to each other when initially meeting and when parting. Following the encounters students discuss the encounter, participants and onlookers. Discussion can be about how each person felt during the exercise (respected, uncomfortable), whether the encounter looked respectful, and how people from other cultures might respond. The discussion may reveal that students sometimes feel "funny" manifesting courtesy (e.g., saying "please" to a peer), but that other students don't think it sounds "funny." This exercise allows students to practice courteous behavior, watch it being modeled by peers, and sets expectations of proper behavior. Do this with different cultures in mind.

Courtesy in different cultures. Students gather information about different cultures in the community, their patterns of courtesy, and the source of these patterns. Students ask for help from community members in learning the ways to be courteous, then practice the different ways and write about using them in real life. This exercise may be conducted in conjunction with "Respectful Encounters." **Assess** with a knowledge test or role plays.

Group unity. Students engage in activities that build trust and interdependence like a ropes course or a group project (non-competitive games can be used here). Remind them of their role as one of a group and supporter of the others. Assess through group reflection after the activity and a self-rating of participation.

Showing respect under difficult circumstances. Have students practice different scenarios in which showing respect is more difficult than usual. Set up scenarios where one would prefer to be cruel or mean to the other person by calling them names or attacking them: (1) arguing with a friend or family member about something you want that they won't give you; (2) someone gets in front of you in line; (3) someone is talking loudly at in a movie theatre; (4) someone is calling a friend of yours names; (5) an adult mistreats you; (6) someone takes credit for something you have done. **Assess** with essays or role plays.

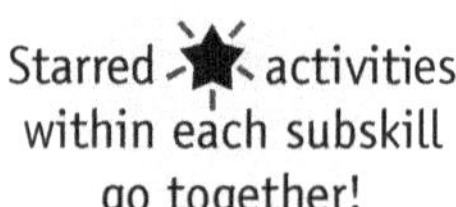
Starred activities
within each subskill
go together!

Respecting Others by Being Civil & Courteous
Ideas for Developing Skills

Level 3 (continued)

Civility in the media. Students analyze evidence for civility or its opposite in a particular medium (television, movies, music, comic books, advertising). The students discuss how to have an influence on the media (write letters to stations, advertisers). Students may be aware of the negative influence of the media and may need encouragement to find examples of respect and courtesy. **Assess** with students actually writing and sending letters to advertisers or station directors.

Level 4: Integrate Knowledge and Procedures
Execute plans, Solve problems

Civility in practice. Students sign a pledge to be civil in particular ways for a week (preferably an area of weakness or ignorance). They select a judge of their behavior (like an older student or adult friend) who monitors how well they do over the time period. Judge looks for improvement.

Creating a courteous school. Students observe the staff and other students in the hallways, lunchroom, other classes and elsewhere. They record how courtesy was or was not displayed. (If necessary, students first brainstorm about how courtesy should be displayed by students and school staff.) Students discuss their observations. Then students take action with one of the following: (1) write an article about their observations for the school newspaper or report them at a school assembly; (2) write a skit on courtesy to be presented at a school assembly; (3) draft a school policy on displaying courtesy; (4) teach other students about how courtesy should be displayed in school. **Assess** with completion of projects.

Coaching for courtesy and civility. Have students coach a new (younger) student from another culture about what is polite and civil in their new school. Discuss a list of things the coach should discuss and demonstrate and practice with the new student. Have students keep track of the results in a journal.

Be Civil and Courteous

Essays or Oral Reports. Have students write an essay or give an oral report about what they've learned.

Quiz. Give a factual test on critical information that they learned.

Project. Assess a project activity in which students take action to promote civility (e.g., letters to politicians, park clean-up, etc.).

Role Plays. Have the students write a skit and act out the roles of the characters demonstrating what they've discussed and learned about civility.

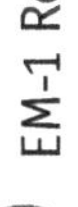

Respecting Others by Being Non-Violent

Creative and Expert Implementer
Real-Life Example

Mahatma Gandhi demonstrated expert skills in creating new approaches to resolving disagreements using various acts of civil non-cooperation. He was trying to persuade Britain to remove itself from its control of India as a colony without using any form of violence. One time he walked 240 miles across the country; many times he fasted until disputes were resolved.

Ideas for Developing Skills

Level 1: Immersion in Examples and Opportunities

Attend to the big picture, Learn to recognize basic patterns

What is non-violence? (1) Invite a person who practices non-violence to speak to the class (they may be from a religious order or a non-profit organization). Ask them to discuss and distinguish violence from non violence. (2) Have students research non-violence and what it means on a day-to-day basis.

What is peacemaking? Show examples of peacemaking in the world (tearing down of the Berlin wall, Nelson Mandela and the reorganization of South Africa). Students reflect on the characteristics of a peacemaker. Discuss who have been peacemakers in their lives, families, etc.

Peacemaking in action. Invite peace activists or others who promote peace (e.g., Buddhists) to speak to the class about their traditions, what they do and why.

Examine those places where peacemaking is needed. Have the students find examples of places, situations, domestic and international conflicts, where peacemaking is needed. What is the root of the problem in each case? What can be done to remedy the contentious, perhaps violent, situation?

How do we maintain peace in our lives? Have the students interview family members (or elders in the community) about how peace is maintained in their homes, e.g., rules, chores, honoring parents, etc. Who intervenes in conflicts at home? At school? Who among their friends would they describe as a peacemaker? Why?

Positive conflict. Have students research the history of peaceful civil disobedience and describe its benefits in comparison to violence. Assess by asking students to make two lists, one of positive conflict, the other of negative.

Starred activities within each subskill go together!

Respecting Others by Being Non-Violent

Ideas for Developing Skills

Level 2: Attention to Facts and Skills

Focus on detail and prototypical knowledge, Build knowledge

Noticing violence and non-violence. Using a list of characteristics or behaviors related to non-violence, have students keep a record of which they observe during the week. They can journal or present a report to class.

Non-violent civil disobedience. Students identify realistic social problems for which civil disobedience might be a worthwhile approach to awakening citizen concern and fostering change.

Conduct research on programs that promote peacemaking methods. Investigate negotiating and conflict resolution skills that might be used to facilitate peacemaking. Have the students seek out different programs which might further peacemaking. How might they apply to problems in relationships with others? With family?

Peacemaking in everyday life. For a week, students identify peacemaking opportunities in television stories, books, their own experiences. **Assess** with a report on what they've observed.

Investigate steps toward peacemaking. Encourage the students to brainstorm about the steps necessary to bring peace to a contentious situation, e.g. bring the parties together, insure that they listen to one another, avoid expressions of anger and resentment, etc.

Peace in literature and poetry. Have the students seek out works of literature or poetry which highlight the importance and the virtue of peace. Give them the opportunity to share it (or a portion of it) with the class and explain why they chose that particular work.

Investigate the role of law in maintaining peace. Students should consider how laws, from local to international, further the maintenance of peace in our local communities, our nation and the world.

Invite guests who have experienced conflict. Have the students invite exchange students (from countries that have experienced conflict or stuggle) or veterans to speak of their experience of war or conflict. Ask the guests to reflect on the value of peace and the importance of peacemaking. Have the students write an essay on the importance of being peacemakers.

Awareness of global non-violence (Obsatz, 2000).
Learn how people in diverse countries and cultures live and see the world. Use resources like the Center for Global Education, Augsburg College, 2211 Riverside Ave., Minneapolis, MN 55454 (612-330-1159). How do the groups view violence? What kinds of violence do they suffer from? What is its cause? How can a person intervene?

Starred activities within each subskill go together!

Respecting Others by Being Non-Violent

Ideas for Developing Skills

Level 2 (continued)

Gather perspectives on war and peace (Obsatz, 2000).
(1) Study the lives of peacemakers such as Ruth Youngdahl Nelson, Oscar Romero (San Salvador), Gandhi (India), Dietrich Bonhoeffer (Germany) Martin Luther King Jr., Aun San Suu Kyi (Burma/Myanmar), Dorothy Day, Jesus, local community members.
(2) Check out organizations such as the Families Against Violence Network, the Institute for Peace and Justice (4144 Lindell Blvd, #408, St. Louis 63108; 314-533-4445), Coop America, and discuss their principles.
(3) Check out publications that promote peace and non-violence (see the Appendix) and report on what kind of topics they cover.

How is the consumer connected to peaceful business practices (or not)? Discuss how consumer choices support corporate practices. Research the practices of corporations that make the products you buy. Where do they get their raw materials? Where are the materials manufactured? How are they transported? How fair are their labor practices (e.g., fair wages, fair work hours)? How much packaging do they use? Is the packaging recyclable? Do they cause harm in their practices? If so, how do they remedy it?

Level 3: Practice Procedures

Set goals, Plan steps of problem solving, Practice skills

Non-violent lifestyle. Students read about people who dedicate their lives to non-violence. Students examine their own lives with the criteria used by these people. **Assess** with an essay comparing two people.

Practicing and using peacemaking statements. Students practice saying peacemaking statements that they can use when conflict arises around them. Students identify opportunities to use them. Statements include: "Take it easy," "It's no big deal," "Let's go," "Cool it," etc.

Class meetings. Use class meetings as a vehicle for practicing peaceful resolution strategies. These can be regularly scheduled and/or held when a conflict arises. Unless students are skilled in self-government, the class meetings should be led by teachers. For best results, they should last usually two minutes on a consistent basis.

Become a peace activist (Obsatz, 2000). Ask students (perhaps one among other choices) to participate in a local peace action by doing one of the following: (1) Ask the students to write a letter, or call and meet an elected official to express their opinions. (2) Join peace vigils, rallies actions and marches. (3) Protest war toys or excessive violence in movies, TV, or video games.

Starred ★ activities within each subskill go together!

Respecting Others by Being Non-Violent

Ideas for Developing Skills

Level 3 (continued)

Organize a peace day for the school (Obsatz, 2000).
Have students organize and implement a day with videos, guest speakers, panels, or join activist activities such as delivering peace flyers to local neighborhoods.

Level 4: Integrate Knowledge and Procedures
Execute plans, Solve problems

Be a peacemaker! Choose to be conscious of the ways that you can bring peace to a situation at home or at school. Within the next week take the opportunity to be the peacemaker in a conflict. **Assess** by reporting back to the class about the experience.

Using peacemaking. Students identify one type of situation in which they will practice peacemaking during the week. This can be at home intervening in a conflict between siblings or seeking peace in a school setting. Practice and report on the outcome, difficulties and successes.

Fostering peace through pen pals. Give the students the opportunity to form pen pal relationships with students from other countries and cultures. Encourage discussion about how communicating with others can foster ongoing peace between individuals and nations.

Cultivate a peaceful lifestyle. Each student identifies ways that they can change their lifestyle to become more of a peacemaker. Students make a strategic plan for doing this (what end result am I aiming for, what are the steps I need to take to get there) and implement the plan. Have them report on their progress and use the class as a support group for the changes.

Teaching others about peaceful living. Have students set up a meeting to help others learn a peaceful lifestyle. You can use videos from the Center for Media Literacy (4727 Wilshire Blvd Suite 403 LA 90010 800-226-9494) or invite speakers, read poems, or present role plays.

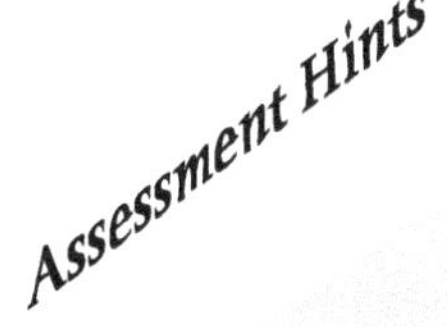

Be Non-violent

Essays or Oral Reports. Have students write an essay or give an oral report about what they've learned about peacemaking and who is a particularly good example of it in their lives.

Interview. Assess an interview by having the students report back to the class, either in a written report or orally, what they talked about and learned from the interview with an exemplary peacemaker.

Individual Performance. Following a cooperative or class activity targeting an issue related to peacemaking, assess students on their individual contribution and performance.

Creative and Expert Implementer Real-Life Example

Respecting Others by Showing Reverence

Albert Schweitzer, a gifted doctor and musician, moved to Africa to help the less fortunate. He was compelled by his love for humanity to give all of his energy to assisting those in Africa who were in need of his expertise. He had so much respect for life that he would not even swat mosquitoes.

Ideas for Developing Skills

Level 1: Immersion in Examples and Opportunities
Attend to the big picture, Learn to recognize basic patterns

Individual worth. Discuss the uniqueness and value of every individual life form, from a snowflake to child. (1) Distribute one peanut-in-its-shell (or orange or other fruit that varies visibly across individuals) to each student. Tell the students that they must get to know their own individual peanut. Draw it. Write down its unique characteristics. Feel it with eyes closed. (Give it a name.) (2) Then collect the peanuts in one (or two) dishes. Students must determine which peanut was theirs. They should exhibit some affection/loyalty to this piece of creation for at least the remainder of that week. **Assess** by having them write a report on the importance of the peanut for human kind.

Care for the environment. Discuss what humans require from their environment (air, water, food). Discuss what can go wrong with these things and how to guard them. What responsibility do we have to those who will come after us years from now, decades from now, centuries from now?

Control waste generation. (1) Have students measure how much waste the school generates in a day or a week. Have them investigate what happens to it. (2) Have students measure how much waste they generate in a week. Have them investigate what happens to it. (3) Have them work on reducing the amount of waste they create, keeping track of how it decreases and why.

What is the status of the local environment? Invite local environmentalists to discuss the status of the local environment. Ask them to describe what they measure and how they measure it, and what affects the findings. You can relate these to health issues, economic issues, or political issues.

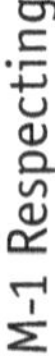

Starred activities within each subskill go together!

Respecting Others by Showing Reverence

Ideas for Developing Skills

Level 2: Attention to Facts and Skills

Focus on detail and prototypical examples, Build knowledge

Respecting human life. Discuss how people show respect for human life. Interview community members about this. In what ways do people disagree and why? Have the student consider his or her views on the issue of respect for human life, whether through a written report or journal entries.

Signs of respect for the earth. Foster a class discussion about the ways in which we show respect for the earth. How can we better express our respect for nature? What can the class do to show its appreciation for the earth? **Assess** by having students write a report on ways they could better respect the earth.

Focus on a particular domain. Students identify the features within a domain that draw wonder from the people in that domain (e.g., biologists and the cell, physicists and the atom).

What is your impact on the world? (1) Stuff. Ask students to itemize everything (or a subset) they own (or use) in terms of one or more of the following: (a) Where does it originate (ingredients, too)? (b) Where did you get it? (c) Why do you have it? (d) What did it cost (in terms of environment, labor, transportation)? (2) Sound. (a) Invite a community musician to discuss the sound aesthetics of one's environs. (b) Discuss examples of noisy and quiet environments (e.g., television blaring vs. listening to rain on window). (c) Discuss with students how they contribute to or decrease noise pollution. (d) Discuss how people can make the world less polluted by sounds. Check out the Noise Pollution Clearinghouse on the web. (3) Aesthetics. (a) Invite a community artist to discuss the aesthetics of one's environs. (b) Discuss examples of ugly and beautiful environments (e.g., flower beds in a corner empty lot versus piles of garbage). (c) Discuss with students how they contribute to making things ugly or beautiful. (d) Discuss how people can make things more beautiful.

History of a basic need. Have students select a project in which they examine the history of one of our basic needs (e.g., clean air, clean water, clean food, shelter). This can be from a North American standpoint, U.S. standpoint, or human world history. What resources are used to meet the basic need? Is the need being met responsibly? Is the need being met universally? What are the various ways this need could be met? Is one better than another?

Don't be a creep (ideas from Halberstam, 1993). Have students role play being a creep and being its opposite, showing reverence and respect for others. (Creeps are persons who are oblivious to their effect on the world and are self-centered. They have no respect for other people, their feelings, opinions or viewpoints. Creeps think what they own is the best, what they do is the best, what they think is the best. They think they know the truth. They also think they are cool.)

Respecting Others by Showing Reverence

Ideas for Developing Skills

Level 2 (continued)

What are the ways that people harm the natural world and the reasons they do?
(1) After an introductory reading or film, discuss the ways that humans harm the natural world. Identify ways to avoid causing these harms.
(2) Interview community members about what they think are the ways people harm the natural world and why. (Reasons could include: ignorance, insensitivity, laziness, pleasure, survival, greed, belief system—e.g., the world is ending, God will take care of it). Have students report on their interviews and synthesize this information with what else they have learned about the environment.

Level 3: Practice Procedures

Set goals, Plan steps of problem solving, Practice skills

Respect for the environment. Discuss conservation generally or for a specific area of work (e.g., food service, woodworking). How can we better reduce, reuse, and recycle our resources? How do we show respect for our environment? The class makes a plan for how to do this and how to measure progress. The class monitors success.

Creating a poster demonstrating respect for the environment (from Dotson & Dotson, 1997). Have the class or small groups create a large poster representing the environment, include the words "Reduce," "Reuse," and "Recycle." Around those words show pictures of ways to do each. Assess by observing participation and by quality of poster.

What do you do with old stuff? Discuss what students and their families do with things they don't want/can't use anymore. Discuss alternative forms of 'recycling' the things. Have students design and carry out a project in which old stuff is collected and 'recycled' (e.g., auctioned off as a fundraiser for a just cause, transported to a charitable organization, sold at a 'garage' sale fundraiser, traded, given to the needy).

Buying new stuff. Discuss how often students and their families buy new things (e.g., clothes, furnishings, appliances). Discuss why the purchase is made (e.g., broken, to have the latest model, to keep up with the neighbors) and whether the reason is a good reason.

What is reverence? Have students investigate the meaning of reverence and then write all the definitions, with illustrations if possible, on a large newsprint. Ideas about reverence from Zukav (1989): Reverence is an attitude of honoring life, of believing that life is valuable for its own sake. Reverence is not respect because respect is a judgment. It is possible to respect one person and not another. But if you revere one person, you revere all persons.

Respecting Others by Showing Reverence
Ideas for Developing Skills

Level 3 (continued)

Respecting our senses. Have students select a project that tries to remedy a situation that disrespects our senses. Here are some examples: (a) hearing: loud music, loud motors, loud advertising; (b) taste: processed foods, contaminated foods, genetically altered foods; (c) sight: light pollution; urban decay, littered roadways; (d) touch: artificial materials; (e) smell: barbecuing, burning wood or other things.

Why are people so indifferent to taking care of the planet? (1) Have students investigate this question (a) in the library, on the internet, (b) by interviewing community members, (c) by conducting anonymous surveys of classes. (2) Discuss the question with students based on the source material they collected. (3) Ask students to develop a campaign to convince other students of the importance of taking care of the planet. (4) Ask students to develop a pledge for students in the school to sign about taking care of the planet.

Level 4: Integrate Knowledge and Procedures
Execute plans, Solve problems

I respect human life. Each student identifies ways that he or she can respect human life and sets detailed and attainable goals to do so, whether through interviews with elders, or reports on visits to nurseries or elder care homes. Students implement their plans. **Assess** with a report on implemented plan.

I respect creation. Each student identifies ways that he or she can respect creation and sets detailed and attainable goals to do so, whether through the cleaning of a local park or roadside or building a bird house. Students implement their plans. **Assess** with a report on implemented plan.

Everyday pollution. Discuss what pollution is, what kinds there are, and what causes it. Have students interview others about how they pollute and figure out how they pollute themselves. Put the information together and have a discussion about remedies. Put together an action plan for making changes in behavior. Implement the plan.

Mentor younger children about eco-living. Have students work with younger children on raising awareness about recycling, clean living, conservation (water, trees, biodiversity). Have the pairs come up with a project to improve the school or community. Select one project from those suggested by cross-age pairs, and have the groups carry it out.

Show Reverence

Essays or Oral Reports. Have students write an essay or give an oral report about what they've learned, or how they intend to implement a plan to improve classroom/school environment.

Posters. Assess by having the students, individually or in small groups, create a poster representing what they've learned.

Individual Performance. Following a cooperative or class activity targeting an issue related to respecting others, assess students on their individual contribution and performance.

Create a Climate
to Develop Respecting Others

- Encourage children to understand and respond positively to emotions in others.
- Promote pro-social action.
- Promote the honoring of rights.
- Develop a sense of responsibility to the group (in the class, in the school).
- Expect honesty, courtesy and regard for others.
- Role model honesty, courtesy and regard for others.
- Emphasize peaceful interactions in the classroom. Don't tolerate violence of any kind.

Bulletin Board Idea: Draw a large video camera or movie reel with the film coming out of it. On the film, have squares with the ethical skills that you are focussing on during that lesson/week/term. (Dotson & Dotson, 1997)

Put "Respect" in the middle of a large bulletin board. Around the word, put pictures or drawings of the different people students need to respect, such as parents, grandparents, teachers, each other, bus drivers, brothers and sisters, and others. (Dotson & Dotson, 1997)

Use a large poster representing the environment. Add the words "Reduce," "Reuse," and "Recycle" and show pictures of ways to do each. Use the header, "Do we respect our environment?" (Dotson & Dotson, 1997)

DO THESE THINGS
when you witness bullying or other interpersonal violence:

Deal with the situation IMMEDIATELY.
State that such abuse is HARMFUL and will not be tolerated.
VALUE the feelings of others by listening with sensitivity.
SUPPORT the victim.
TAKE ASIDE those involved to discuss the incident.
APPLY APPROPRIATE CONSEQUENCES to the offender.
EXAMINE THE CONTEXT for subtle support of such offenses.

DON'T DO THESE THINGS
when you witness bullying or other interpersonal violence:

Don't IGNORE it, let it pass unchallenged, or let intangible fear block your ability to act.
Don't OVERREACT with a put-down of the offender.
Don't IMPOSE CONSEQUENCES until you know what happened from everyone involved.
Don't focus entirely on the offender; REMEMBER THE VICTIM.
Don't EMBARRASS either party publicly.
Don't ASSUME THE INCIDENT IS ISOLATED from the context in which it occurred.

Selections to Post in the Classroom
For Respecting Others

"Don't put off for tomorrow what you can do today, because if you enjoy it today you can do it again tomorrow." –James A. Michener (as cited in Dotson & Dotson, 1997)

Place a clock in the center of the board with the header, "Don't merely count your days—Make your days count." (as cited in Dotson & Dotson, 1997)

Post a checklist of the characteristics your students use to describe a trustworthy person under the header, "What does it mean to be trustworthy?"

Sample Student Self-Monitoring

Respecting Others

Encourage active learning by having students learn to monitor their own learning

Be Civil and Courteous

When I want to treat someone I don't like with respect, I focus on...
What I remember about how to respect people in this situation...
How do I verify that I am being respectful of this person?
I honor and respect elders.
I do not say bad things about others.
I listen to others.
I get along with people who are different from me.
I respect people's time.
I respect people's space.
I groom myself well.

Be Non-violent

I do not force others to do what I want.
I am gentle with others.
I try to end fights, not start them.
I look at the bright side of things.
I make conscious decisions about living peacefully in the world.
I think about how to help others with non-violence.

Show Reverence

I take charge of my health and make healthy choices.
I avoid things that can harm me.
I treat people with respect.
I take care to recycle what I can.
I think about respecting the natural world frequently.
I know how to respect the natural world.
I am aware of my impact on the natural world.
I consciously try to respect other people.
I try to read others for cues about how they want to be treated.

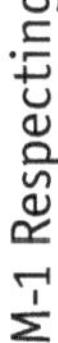

Cultivating Conscience

(Develop Conscience)

WHAT

Conscience is the driving force behind self command and temperance. A sense of conscience is the sense of discomfort, based on a sense of empathy, that one experiences upon realizing the harm, or potential harm, that one may inflict on others. A person of honor has developed skills to control impulses and manage power.

WHY

In order to take ethical action, a person's sense of what is right and wrong must be accompanied by a sense of conscience. This motivation in conscience, this empathic understanding, will better equip a person to maintain ethical goals even under adverse conditions.

SUBSKILLS OVERVIEW

1: Self Command

- Impulse control
- Temperance

2: Manage Influence and Power

- Seeking to avoid extremism

3: Be Honorable

- Trustworthiness
- Honesty
- Genuineness
- Gratitude

Web Wise

The Peace Corps' World Wise Schools has resources and ideas for global education: www.peacecorps.gov/wws

See www.rippleeffects.com for youth oriented information about personal effects on others

For lesson plans and guidelines on many aspects of character: www.goodcharacter.com

Cultivating Conscience through Self Command

Creative and Expert Implementer Real-Life Example

Daunte Culpepper, the quarterback for the Minnesota Vikings, is able to remain cool under pressure, a remarkable achievement for a young quarterback. His self command extends to how he treats others. He is very respectful of others, and highly regarded by players, coaches and sports reporters for his remarkable courtesy on and off the field, even in adverse situations.

Ideas for Developing Skills

Level 1: Immersion in Examples and Opportunities

Attend to the big picture, Learn to recognize basic patterns

Observations of developing self command. Have students observe young children and how they do and do not control themselves. **Assess** by having students turn in a checklist of observations.

The consequences of having no self command (Dotson & Dotson, 1997). (1) Discuss persons who have failed to develop a healthy self command. For example, many convicts acted impulsively when they committed their crime. (2) Discuss examples of persons who no longer have control over their lives. Ask students how they would feel if they were in prison or confined to a bed. (3) Help students identify the advantages of developing a healthy self-command. **Assess** by having students write a paragraph on what they've learned regarding self-command.

List of television/cartoon characters and their levels of self command. Have the students gather in groups to consider different television characters, animated or otherwise, who display varying levels of self command. What consequences does a lack of self command have in the instances where it appears? **Assess** by having groups present their lists to the class and explain their reasoning.

Self command at work. Students interview working people asking about the situations in their work that require self-control, how they manage it, what the consequences are if they don't.

What is temperance? Identify examples of temperance in stories and film. Have a discussion of where they practice temperance in their lives and/or observe it in others. **Assess** by observing quality and frequency of contributions.

Starred activities within each subskill go together!

Cultivating Conscience through Self Command

Ideas for Developing Skills

Level 1 (continued)

Examining extremes. Show students examples of people behaving in extreme ways. Have them, as individuals or in groups, find more examples from different domains (i.e., political, religious, comedic, etc.). Discuss the dangers.

Temperance at work or study. Discuss with students how people demonstrate temperance within different areas of study (e.g., mathematics, biology) or work (e.g., police work, teaching, professional football) by (1) inviting a member of the profession to speak to the class on this topic; (2) finding examples in news and media; (3) having students interview a professional; (4) having students conduct research.

Level 2: Attention to Facts and Skills

Focus on detail and prototypical examples, Build knowledge

Courtesy rules as they relate to self command. Set courtesy rules in class and write about, discuss, and/or debate how these rules relate to self command and why they are important. Post courtesy rules to establish a clear message as to what is acceptable and how it is an important facet of every interaction. The practice of posted courtesy is particularly relevant to the development of a healthy self command and conscience as students can refer to the posted rules as they decide what actions to execute and what impulses to control. In short, having posted courtesy rules makes explicit what should be implicit in an ethical classroom and thus serves as an aide in having these rules internalized, without embarrassment or badgering from the teacher. **Assess** by observing and recording level of participation and contribution of each student.

"Restraint is an infusion of thinking—and thoughtfulness—into everything we do. We choose the behavior that, although it may not seem the most gratifying now, will make us feel good five minutes from now, tomorrow, or next year. Restraint is the art of feeling good later." (Forni, 2002, p. 23)

Essay writing and discussion of conscience. Students write about conscience with the guidance of "thought provoking questions" (e.g. "What is conscience?") followed by a class discussion. Students write about the origin of conscience—where it comes from and why it exists. Lickona (1991) lists six questions to have students discuss or write about:

1. What is conscience?
2. Does everybody have one?
3. When does your conscience appear?
4. Do you listen to your conscience?
5. Which do you consider conscience: an enemy or a friend?
6. What advice would you give to other people about their conscience?

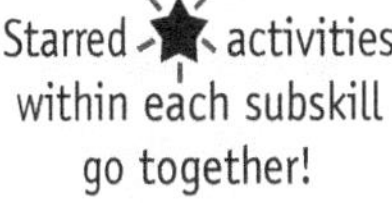
Starred activities within each subskill go together!

Cultivating Conscience through Self Command

Ideas for Developing Skills

Level 2 (continued)

Stories about self command. Use a story that highlights self-command (or its lack). Have the students discuss the implications of not staying within one's bounds. Discussion should pay particular attention to the positive aspects of self command and how one can work on improving his or her ability.

Athletes and self command (Dotson & Dotson, 1997). Talk about athletes and how they become good enough to get their million-dollar jobs. When top athletes have these good jobs, can they quit? What happens when athletes fail to exercise their self command? Point out that self command is learned, just as athletic training is learned. **Assess** by brainstorming about those athletes who exhibit a well developed self command; and those who do not.

Temperance in the media (Dotson & Dotson, 1997). Brainstorm with the class about characters in the media, animated or otherwise, who show temperance and avoid extremes. Make two lists: first, of those who show temperance, and then of those who do not. What difference does it make in the lives of the characters?

Identify benefits of temperance on health. Identify foods that represent healthy choices, and discuss how eating poorly versus not eating well affects behavior. At the outset, they will probably not make the connection. Ask them to track through a health journal "how good they feel" and see if eating has any effect on them. **Assess** by collecting the health journal each month.

Discussion of choices for and against temperance. Brainstorm with the class about instances when students have valued temperance by their choices and when they have not. **Assess** by asking students to make a list of their responses.

Level 3: Practice Procedures

Set goals, Plan steps of problem solving, Practice skills

Identify strategies for avoiding temptation (Dotson & Dotson, 1997). Identify strategies for avoiding the temptation to respond inappropriately, such as: counting to 10, going for a walk, thinking about the consequences, and trying to identify what the other person is feeling. Have students practice these techniques. Assess by having the students journal about when they have used these strategies.

Starred ★ activities within each subskill go together!

Cultivating Conscience through Self Command

Ideas for Developing Skills

Level 3 (continued)

Essay on impulse control. Students write an essay recalling a time when they had to exercise impulse control. They should explain the positive outcome, the difficulty in following through, the method they used to stay on task, and the possible negative outcomes had they not had such control. Likewise, students could write an essay about the consequences of a character who did not control his or her impulses. **Assess** by conducting a class discussion about how impulse control enhances the good order of the classroom.

Consider examples in one's own life. Have students consider the ways in which they exercise self command in their own lives, particularly regarding their treatment of other people. When has self command served them well? When have they failed to exercise it? **Assess** with a report.

Practicing self command. Everyone has an area to work on in terms of self control (e.g., eating junk food, getting angry, yelling at others, watching too much television). Have students identify their weak areas and practice curtailing for a week. **Assess** with journal on the experience and progress.

An interview with an adult mentor. Have the student interview someone who knows the student well. First, have the student inquire of the mentors own experience of self command in the workplace and at home. Secondly, have the student ask the mentor to list the ways in which he observes self command in the student. **Assess** with a report.

Define the difference between "aggressive" and "assertive" (Dotson & Dotson, 1997). Spend time discussing the meaning of and differences between being aggressive and being assertive. Ask students to list in two columns occasions when they have been each. Discuss ways of getting the point across without being pushy or losing control. **Assess** by collecting the self-reports of their aggressive/assertive behavior.

Keep a log of food choices. As a means of heightening self-awareness and temperance commit to eating healthy foods for one week, log food choices and note those that satisfy the commitment and those that do not. **Assess** by having them turn in their logs for review.

Starred activities within each subskill go together!

Cultivating Conscience through Self Command

Ideas for Developing Skills

Level 3 (continued)

Temperance in response to peer pressure (from Dotson & Dotson, 1997). Discuss how temperance is important especially in the face of peer pressure. Identify strategies for maintaining a sound conscience in the face of peer pressure. Examples could include avoiding smoking, drinking, excessive teasing, etc. **Assess** by having the students do a self-evaluation of their temperance in the face of peer pressure and a personal mission statement articulating how they intend to do better.

Role play peer pressure challenges to temperance. Conduct role-plays of various peer pressure situations, such as saying 'no' to smoking, drinking, etc. Other role plays such as studying for a test even when everyone else is talking, or avoiding teasing when others are doing it.

Level 4: Integrate Knowledge and Procedures

Execute plans, Solve problems

Practicing self command with things. Tally how many and what kind of possessions students own. Tally how many times students go shopping each week/month to buy new things. Tally how many times students manage or worry about their possessions each week. After making a tally, ask students to cut back on purchases, and give some things away, as a way to practice control over their actions.

Fasting from technology. Have students fast from a favorite technological device (or all of them) for one day or more and keep a journal—write every 30-60 minutes about feelings and desires and actions. Ask students to try to last as long as they can without the device. Report on the experience. Encourage students to do this regularly (like a food fast).

Teaching temperance to younger students. Establish a mentoring program where students teach younger students the meaning of temperance and ways in which to exercise it. **Assess** by asking the pairs of students to present to the class what they have learned through the experience.

Starred activities within each subskill go together!

Assessment Hints

Self Command

Essays or Oral Reports. Have students write an essay or give an oral report about what they've learned about self command and who is a particularly good example of it in their lives.

List of Exemplars. Assess by having the students, individually or in small groups, create a list of those from television or movies who have demonstrated impressive self command and those who have not.

Journaling. Over a period of time, have students record observations of their own, and others' skills with regard to self command, both positively and negatively.

Cultivating Conscience by Managing Influence & Power

In the United States, there is an unwritten rule followed by ***former presidents***—that former presidents avoid criticizing presidents in office. Criticism is viewed as partisan and not in the national interests. It is considered a sign of respect and leadership for presidents to temper their influence by going along with this rule.

Creative and Expert Implementer Real-Life Example

Ideas for Developing Skills

Level 1: Immersion in Examples and Opportunities

Attend to the big picture, Learn to recognize basic patterns

Influential people.
(1) Influential role models. Present examples of living persons in particular domains (e.g., science, politics, religion) who have influence and power but who use it respectfully. Have students identify what the characteristics are of a respectful use of power.
(2) Influential community members and elders. Invite influential community members to class to discuss the power they have and how they use it to bring about more good.
(3) Historical influential figures. Have students investigate historical figures with power: what kind of power did they have and how did they use it? How did it improve the world? How did they bring about more good?

Getting and using influence in a domain. Select a domain (e.g., science, one of the arts, politics, business) and have students investigate one or more of the following: (1) What does it mean to have power in this domain (what does it look like)? (2) How do people get power in this domain? (3) Who has power in this domain? (4) How do people use their power in this domain? (5) Where and when is power used? (6) Are power and influence the same thing?

Jeer messages. Present or have students find examples of messages that ridicule the person and avoid addressing the issue. This is a technique used to suppress minority voices on many topics. Many talk-radio shows use this ploy to play on the bigotry of their audiences to persuade the audience of their viewpoint while not having to reason about issues.

Examine messages about women and minorities. (1) Show students "Killing me softly" or a similar film about how advertising conveys false and unrealistic standards for women's beauty, or the characteristics of a minority group(s). (2) Have students find examples of misleading advertising and television/movie roles and actions that put women and minorities "in their place." These media have influence. Research shows that repeated viewing of R-rated slasher films decreases empathy for victims of rape (citations in Pratkanis & Aronson, 1992); after television was introduced to a country recently (where female ideal beauty was plumpness), girls started developing eating disorders.

Cultivating Conscience by Managing Influence & Power

Ideas for Developing Skills

Level 2: Attention to Facts and Skills

Focus on detail and prototypical examples, Build knowledge

Study powerful individuals. Study particular influential persons and how they used their power and influence respectfully. How do they share power? How do they stay powerful without harming others?

International influence. Study the influence of the U.S. in the world in a particular area, today or in the past. Does/did the U.S. use its power respectfully? How does/did it bring about more good in the world?

Figuring out power. Discuss one or more of the questions listed below and then complete one of the following activities. (1) Have students find examples of the topic(s) in literature, movies and television, history, current events, or in the local setting. Report to class on the findings. (2) Invite a group of adults from different walks of life to speak about power issues. (3) Role play interactions between those with power and those without.

(a) What kinds of power are there? *Individual power* enables you to mobilize yourself to accomplish things, and can include circumstantial power, which comes from a certain role a person has at the moment, and perceptual power—the power we grant to others and the power they grant to us in our interactions. *Group power* is that which arises when we join with others to work to accomplish something we cannot do alone. *Interpersonal power* is the power to influence others. *Social power* is power over groups of people and to enforce control. Ask students to identify the kinds of power they have or could have if they joined together.

(b) Who has power? Show examples of and discuss the types of power people can have over others. We can give our power to people who can reward or punish us. We give power to experts and to legitimate authorities. Who are the legitimate authorities you give power to? Who are illegitimate authorities you give power to?

(c) How is power exchanged? Power is exchanged willingly or coercively. You give your power willingly to the bus driver who gets you where you want to go. Unwillingly perhaps, you give your power to people in charge. Have you been coerced to do something? How did it feel? Have you coerced someone else to do something? What is a better way to get along than coercion?

(d) How is power used? Ask students to investigate how people use power? How is it used for ill and how is it used for good? Have them study the elements of using power for good. Discuss whether they can use the power they have for good and how.

(e) What is an abuse of power? Ask students to investigate how people can abuse power in personal relationships (couples, parent/child, friends, siblings), at work, in government, or in business.

Cultivating Conscience by Managing Influence & Power

Ideas for Developing Skills

Level 2 (continued)

Is it okay for the big to bully? Discuss whether or not those who are stronger or bigger should have more authority (e.g., males over females, adults over children, big guys over smaller guys, big countries over little countries, humans over animals, humans over plants, abled people over disabled).

Domain influence in practice. Ask a local leader in a particular area of work to come and discuss issues of power and influence in the domain. (Domains include science, writing, fine arts, sport, business, education, craftsmanship.) Ask students to write a report afterwards.

Boomerang life. Have students discuss ideas that run through every religion. (1) Action and corresponding response: (a) You receive from the world what you give to the world. (b) As ye sow so shall ye reap. (c) For every action there is an equal and opposite reaction (third law of motion). (2) What examples of this do I see in the world? (3) How do these ideas apply to my life?

The four strategies of persuasion (Pratkanis & Aronson, 1992, *Age of Propaganda*). Have students examine commercials for the following strategies.

(a) Pre-persuasion: Defining the issue and the decision to be made. A persuader can influence how you think about an issue and get your consent without looking like he/she is persuading you.
(b) Source credibility. The source of the message must be likable or trustworthy or have an attribute that supports the validity of the message.
(c) Focus the receiver's attention away from counterarguments and towards the desired message. Using vivid imagery is one way to do this.
(d) Control the emotions of the receiver. First you arouse the emotions of the receiver and then you present a solution to the emotions.

Cultivating Conscience by Managing Influence & Power

Ideas for Developing Skills

Level 3: Practice Procedures

Set goals, Plan steps of problem solving, Practice skills

Imitate a role model. Have students identify a powerful positive role model. Have them investigate how they use their power respectfully. Have students imitate some positive use of power and keep a journal on it.

Imagine having power or not having power. (1) Have students visualize being the opposite sex as they go through their day. Discuss what kind of power they felt. (2) Have students visualize being a powerful person for a day. (3) Have students visualize being a homeless or powerless person for a day. You may use a relaxation-visualization exercise (see EM-5 relaxation-visualization activity, p. 118) for this. Ask students to write about their experience afterwards.

Tempering influence and power interpersonally. Have students make a list of people they have (or sometimes have) power over. Ask them to describe how they exercise that power. Have them analyze whether or not they exercise it respectfully. Have them think about how to be respectful and have them report on their success after the next time they exercise power with that person.

Tempering the power of the media over you. Present a lesson on media literacy (there are resources on the web). Ask students to keep track of how the media tries to influence them. You may focus on a particular product or particular medium. The class should discuss the results of their research.

Negative and positive words affect others. Like a stone in a pond, our words and actions ripple across the community. Your negative words can deflate the mood of someone else who may in turn do the same to others. You can create a chain reaction of positive or negative relations. Positive actions affect others. Even a smile, encouraging word, or positive attitude can affect another person in profound ways—encouraging them to take risks to help others or discouraging them from reaching out. Have students carry out a brief experiment with their friends. One day the student is negative about everything, another day the student is positive about everything. Students report on how their friends were influenced.

Authentic power. Zukav (1989), in *The Seat of the Soul,* discusses authentic power. The person with authentic power is so strong internally, so empowered, that he/she does not think of using force against another person and is incapable of making a victim out of anyone. Authentic power comes about from aligning our thoughts, emotions, and actions with our highest selves (soul, inner spirit). With authentic power we cherish life and are not afraid. Have students think and write about their highest selves. (a) What is my soul? (b) What does my soul want? (c) How does my soul affect my life? (d) How can I nurture my soul?

Cultivating Conscience by Managing Influence & Power

Ideas for Developing Skills

Level 3 (continued)

Innoculation. Research shows (e.g., Pratkanis & Aronson, 1992) that people are influenced by advertisements (and other messages) even when they know they are being manipulated (for example, when you get to the store you buy the familiar brand—familiar because you have seen many ads for it). One thing that works against the subtle power of messages is innoculation—where the opposite side of the argument is presented to or generated by the receiver. (1) Have the students watch several ads. For each ad student groups develop counter arguments to the explicit and subtle messages. (2) Have students present their arguments to the class and compile them. (3) Have students make posters or presentations about the ads to other students.

Level 4: Integrate Knowledge and Procedures

Execute plans, Solve problems

Tempering influence and power day to day. Have students map out the different ways they influence others and keep a journal as they monitor whether or not they do it respectfully over a period of time (1 week, 1 month). When they come across a situation where they are confused about what is respectful, have the class discuss situations like it and come up with respectful interactions. Have students practice new ways of being respectful. An adult mentor would be an ideal evaluator for this activity.

Tempering interpersonal power cross-culturally and intergenerationally. After studying differences in showing respect cross culturally and inter-generationally, as well as differences in showing power and influence, ask the students to monitor how they do in these situations. Have them work with an older student to increase their appropriate respectful behavior.

Social action against manipulation of children. Take action to protect children from advertising and manipulative messages. Children under age 8 often cannot distinguish fact from fiction.

Cultivating Conscience by Managing Influence & Power

Ideas for Developing Skills

Level 4 (continued)

Offensive against manipulation. If we don't take steps to counter the bombardment of propaganda, we fall prey to it and are controlled by it. Pratkanis and Aronson (1992) suggest several steps individuals should take to lesson the power of the manipulations. (a) Be careful not to fall for the myth that propaganda influences everyone but you. You must realize that you are vulnerable too. (b) Monitor your emotions and ask why the message is making you feel a particular way. (c) Explore the credibility and motivation of the message source. (d) Think rationally about the message. Research shows that we are susceptible to messages that we don't consciously think about. (e) Before you make a decision, consider the range of options. (f) Base your evaluation on the actions of the messenger not the words. (g) Consider whether the information you are hearing is a rumor without foundation. (h) If you are told that 'everyone is doing it,' ask why. (i) Avoid deals that look too good to be true. (j) Always try to find arguments for the other side. (k) Use more than one source of information. (l) Get the news but don't expect it to be entertaining.

Action against propaganda. Pratkanis and Aronson (1992) suggest several steps that citizens can take to move companies away from misleading advertising: (1) Write companies to request proof of advertised claims. (2) Support and extend efforts to squelch deceptive advertising. (3) Support and extend efforts to eliminate misleading labels. (4) Demand consumer affairs shows on television. (5) Promote the institutions of democracy because a "democracy is a pattern of social relations that encourages deliberative persuasion (not propaganda) and respects the rights and responsibilities of all citizens" (p. 348).

Assessment Hints

Manage Influence and Power

Essays or Oral Reports. Have students write an essay or give an oral report about what they've learned about tempering your influence and power and who is a particularly good example of it in their lives.

Individual Performance. Following a cooperative or class activity targeting an issue related to tempering your influence and power, assess students on their individual contribution and performance.

Journaling. Over a period of time, perhaps a week, have students record issues of tempering your influence and power.

Cultivating Conscience by Being Honorable

Creative and Expert Implementer
Real-Life Example

It is easy to think of people who have failed in being honest or trustworthy. It is more difficult to think of people who are honest and trustworthy as a general rule. ***Abraham Lincoln*** is said to have walked many miles to return money after he discovered that he had been given too much change in a store purchase.

Ideas for Developing Skills

Level 1: Immersion in Examples and Opportunities
Attend to the big picture, Learn to recognize basic patterns

Identify honesty. Present a film or read a story and have students identify instances of honesty and dishonesty and their consequences. **Assess** by having students identify instances in a new film or story.

Discuss the definition of trustworthy. Students watch a film or read a story and find instances of trustworthiness. In the discussion, link it to honesty, dependability, and loyalty. How does trustworthiness affect relationships? Who do you most trust in your life? **Assess** with an essay on trustworthiness.

Honesty in different periods in history. Students gather information about honesty in different historical periods. They compare and contrast what areas of life were most important for honesty and what effect dishonesty had on the community. **Assess** through written reports on the information which are presented to the class.

Character story. Have students read about a real person who may work in a particular area of study. Students reflect upon the story of the person and how caring and honesty is related to a general sense of respect one has for another. Students should also indicate and discuss which behaviors in the story exemplify these skills and how they could exemplify these skills in their lives. Assess after discussion with an essay on how students will apply what they've learned.

Exemplars of gratitude in our lives. Have the students brainstorm about the people in their lives for whom they are most grateful. Discuss the things that those people have done for which the students are thankful.

Cultivating Conscience by Being Honorable
Ideas for Developing Skills

Level 1 (continued)

Identifying gratitude. Present students with different video and story scenarios, and ask students to discriminate between gratitude and ingratitude. Have the class discuss the scenarios and point out the ways in which the characters show gratitude.

Gathering examples of expressions of gratitude. Have students find examples of gratitude (1) from books, or the web; (2) from family and community members. Ask them to write up a report on the benefits of being grateful and showing gratitude.

Discuss the many gifts we have in the U.S. (1) Shelter. Describe the shortage of housing in some countries, and how families have to share one room together or a small apartment with other families. How would they feel if another family moved in with them? Ask each student to identify one thing that they are thankful for about their home. (2) Food. Describe the shortage of food in other parts of the world, and that many people go to bed hungry. Have they ever gone to bed hungry? What does/might that feel like? What food/meal are they most grateful for? (3) Clothing. Have they ever been wanting for clothing? Who around them might be in need of clothing? What might cause others to have fewer clothes than them and fewer options of getting them? Do we need all that we have? Do we wear everything in out closets? Might we consider giving away our unused clothing? What is our favorite piece of clothing/outfit? (4) Heat and air-conditioning. Do you have heat and air-conditioning in your home? How often do you use it? Could you live without it? Are there those who do? (5) Entertainment. Have them brainstorm about their entertainment options. To whom are such activities available? What do they most enjoy?

Being honorable in your work. Invite adults from different areas of work (e.g., science, farming, journalism, social service, politics, sport, business, education) and ask them to discuss what being honorable entails in their area of work.

Level 2: Attention to Facts and Skills
Focus on detail and prototypical examples, Build knowledge

Honesty in particular fields. Discuss with students how people demonstrate trustworthiness within different areas of study (e.g., mathematics, biology) or work (e.g., police work, teaching, professional football) by: (1) inviting a member of the profession to speak to the class on this topic; (2) finding examples in news and media; (3) having students interview a professional; (4) having students conduct research.

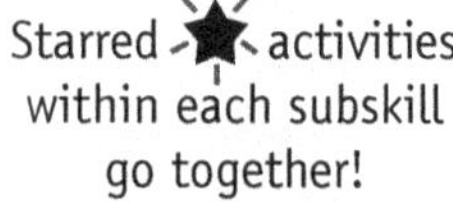
Starred activities within each subskill go together!

Cultivating Conscience by Being Honorable

Ideas for Developing Skills

Level 2 (continued)

Trustworthiness reality check. Invite veterans, judges, former convicts to discuss their experiences. (This must be done very carefully so that violence and deviance are not enhanced in the eyes of the students.) Speakers engage the classroom with stories about decisions people have made and how it impacted the lives of those involved. Having judges or other figures in society engage the class with stories about their experiences can help the students develop a sense of understanding of consequences for unethical behavior to the perpetrator and the victim. From this understanding a sense of respect for others should be enhanced. **Assess** with an essay about reasons to avoid such behavior.

Honesty in different cultures. Students gather information about honesty in the different cultures of their community (through interviews or historical documents) and write up the information in a report they present to the class. They can ask such questions as: When is it important to be honest? What information is private? What kinds of questions will yield untruthful information (due to privacy being more important)? Why is honesty important in the community? What happens/should happen to people who are dishonest? Tell about a time when honesty helped or dishonesty hurt your community. **Assess** by having students present the information to class (you may invite community members) in oral reports, drawings, poems, skits.

Mapping trustworthiness. Spend several lessons examining trustworthiness in different ways and contexts. (1) Types of trust. Interview people in different settings about how people can trust one another (contexts such as home, school, work). How do the situations demand different types of trust? **Assess** with reports on what they've learned. (2) What does a trustworthy person look like (Dotson & Dotson, 1997)? Interview elders, read stories, watch television and develop a list of characteristics of a person who is trustworthy and a person who is not. **Assess** by report. (3) The importance of trustworthiness in a job (Dotson & Dotson, 1997). Invite a speaker from the counseling office to discuss with students the types of careers available and the requirement that employees be trustworthy. **Assess** with reports. (4) Trustworthiness and lasting relationships (Dotson & Dotson, 1997). Locate the latest statistics on marriage and divorce. Discuss these statistics and the importance of trust to long-term relationships. **Assess** by quality of individual contributions. (5) Boundaries of trust. Discuss different kinds of boundaries: relational, social, economic, ethnic. Which should be respected? **Assess** through a report. (6) The importance of trustworthiness. Interview a manager at McDonald's, at a grocery store, or in your neighborhood. Ask the manager how important it is for employees to be trustworthy. **Assess** by having them write up the interview in two paragraphs.

Starred activities within each subskill go together!

Cultivating Conscience by Being Honorable

Ideas for Developing Skills

Level 2 (continued)

The benefits of living in the U.S. (Dotson & Dotson, 1997). Do an in-depth study of one of the areas mentioned in level 1. Discuss the advantages of living in the United States compared to other, perhaps poorer, nations. What opportunities do we know here that those in other countries may not? What are some of the things for which the students are thankful? Brainstorm about ways we could be more grateful. Consider in small groups or in the class as a whole how each person might show more gratitude at home, at school, with friends, with family, etc. Relate this conversation to the times that they themselves have valued gratitude being shown to them by others.

Discuss being grateful for good health (Dotson & Dotson, 1997). Address some of the following questions: Is good health something that students take for granted? Have any of the students had a serious illness or surgery? Do they have a parent or grandparent who is in poor health? How is that person's life affected by poor health?

Discuss service personnel who deserve our thanks (Dotson & Dotson, 1997). Is it important to say "thank you" to someone who is just doing what they are paid to do, such as the janitor, teacher, or cafeteria worker? Ask students to write a short thank you note to someone who works at the school. After you read the notes to make sure they are appropriate, deliver them for your students.

Appreciating that "It's a wonderful life." Have the students watch the film *It's a Wonderful Life* and discuss the things that George Bailey had to be thankful for even though he didn't realize it. Have the students make a list of the things for which they could be grateful.

Level 3: Practice Procedures

Set goals, Plan steps of problem solving, Practice skills

Group trust. Use group strengthening exercises to increase trust and sense of community and respect. **Assess** by monitoring participation and cooperation.

A checklist of trustworthiness (Dotson & Dotson, 1997). Develop a checklist for evaluating the trustworthiness of a person. What criteria would you use to evaluate this characteristic? (You may want to write down how a trustworthy person would respond in a series of situations.) Assess checklists.

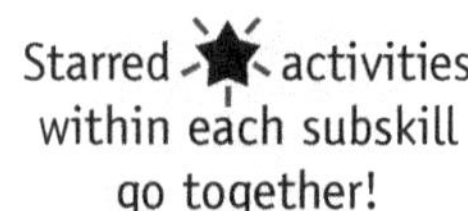
Starred activities
within each subskill
go together!

Cultivating Conscience by Being Honorable

Ideas for Developing Skills

Level 3 (continued)

Rewriting stories for honesty. Students read stories about honesty and then discuss how the characters were honest/dishonest. The discussion could involve talking about honesty as a code, how the characters thought about honesty, and whether the characters acted honestly. **Assess** by having students write a revision of the story where the character is more honest than in the original story; or students can act out the revision in pairs or in groups.

Whom do you know who is trustworthy? (Dotson & Dotson, 1997). Ask the students to identify five persons in their lives whom they think are trustworthy. What are the characteristics that make each of those persons trustworthy? How would they rate their own trustworthiness? How would their friends or parents rate it? **Assess** with a report.

Role play an ethical dilemma (Dotson & Dotson, 1997). Provide students with situations in which they are tempted to be untrustworthy and have them role play different responses. Discuss the ramifications of the choices. **Assess** by observing their participation.

Effects of stealing. Demonstrate how stealing begets stealing with classroom role plays. Discuss with the class some of the negative effects that stealing can have on a classroom community and on society as a whole.

Honesty dilemmas. Presented with a challenging dilemma about honesty (where the truth should be told), students talk about how the dilemma should be resolved and then create an implementation plan, where they then have to role play the actual implementation in small groups. **Assess** with written responses to or role playing a new dilemma.

Honesty in the classroom community. Students discuss different ways dishonesty can damage the classroom community. Students keep track of situations in which students were honest. When these occur, the class discusses why this is beneficial for everyone.

Interview a person about gratitude. Interview a person who emigrated to the U.S. from another country; ask that person if they are thankful to be in the U.S. For what in this country are they particularly thankful? **Assess** with an essay based on the interview.

Practice gratitude. Practice gratitude by having the students write a letter to someone to whom they are grateful. Have them be especially aware of the things that people do for them each day and to keep track of such things for a 24-hour period.

Starred activities within each subskill go together!

Cultivating Conscience by Being Honorable

Ideas for Developing Skills

Level 3 (continued)

Write a note of thanks to the person whom you interviewed. After reflecting on the interview with the person from another country who is living in the U.S. (see level 3 above), have the students write a letter to the person expressing gratitude. The thanks can be for both the time they gave them to do the interview, but also, perhaps, a thank you for heightening their awareness of the things they take for granted.

Be humble. Discuss healthy humility. Humility is not feeling bad about yourself. Humility is not faked. Humility is not the opposite of pride (faked humility is). Pride is putting yourself above others (putting yourself below others might look like humility but it is still pride because you are separating yourself as more special). Humility is a level-headed awareness of what you can and cannot do, an attitude of being one of the team ready to pull together. If you have a talent, you should share it when asked politely (e.g., playing the piano even when you might be a little out of practice). If you hold your talent back, you are being proud and self-centered. Have students identify what talents and skills they have and can share with others.

Level 4: Integrate Knowledge and Procedures

Execute plans, Solve problems

Keeping promises. Assign students to keep track of how many times they make promises and how many times the promises are kept. (1) Students assess themselves daily on how trustworthy each student considers him or herself. Then they write a self-analysis. (2) Students write down the details of times when they did not keep a promise. At the end of the self-assessment period they write an analysis of what makes keeping promises difficult. **Assess** the reports.

Journaling on gratitude. Students reflect and write on personal experiences with gratitude for one week. Ask them to keep track of those things for which they were particularly thankful that week, and what they did to express their gratitude, if anything.

Starred activities within each subskill go together!

Cultivating Conscience by Being Honorable

Ideas for Developing Skills

Level 4 (continued)

Write a story of an ungrateful person. Write a fictional story about an ungrateful person. What implications might it have for the person's life? Cause something to happen in the story that changes this person's attitude. What changes might result?

Shadow an honorable person. Ask local religious, ROTC leaders or veterans (or others pledged to an honor code of one sort or another) to speak in class about honor. Have students shadow volunteers from this group as they make decisions. Prepare guidelines (see sample questions, this page) to help the leaders think aloud while they are making decisions so the students get an idea of what they are thinking and how they apply the honor code. Ask the leaders to coach the students in the thoughtfulness that they have practiced in honoring their codes. After a period of practice and coaching, have students and leaders report on the experience.

Sample Questions to Answer Aloud during Decision-Making

Questions to ponder aloud:
What is the problem?
What is the decision that needs to be made?
How do I know that this is the problem or decision to be solved?
What is the important information I need to look at?
What alternatives do I have?
What are the best and worst reasons for each alternative?
Why do I make the decision I make?

Be Honorable

Essays or Oral Reports. Have students write an essay or give an oral report about what they've learned about being honorable and who is a good exemplar of it in their lives.

Checklist. Give the students the opportunity to come up with a list of the qualities and characteristics that describe an honorable person.

Interview. Assess an interview by having the students report back to the class, either in a written report or orally, what they talked about and learned from the interview.

Role Plays. Have the students write a skit and act out the roles of the characters demonstrating what they've discussed and learned about being honorable.

Creative Writing. Have the students write a story that portrays someone who lives this skill particularly well, and also one that portrays someone who lives it rather poorly.

Journaling. Over a period of time, have students record observations of their own, and others' demonstrations of being honorable, or perhaps those instances where there is an obvious lack of it.

Create a Climate
to Cultivate Conscience

- On a daily basis, discuss personal responsibility to control impulses to get along with others.
- Frequently point out the effects of student behavior on other students, the school community, their families and home communities.
- Model courtesy.
- The teacher should model ethical citizenship.
- Teach skills for active democratic citizenship such as discussing the reasoning behind particular arguments for action.
- Model responsible uses of resources (e.g., don't be wasteful, only take what you need, recycle, etc.).
- Expect responsible resource use. Discuss resource use in particular fields of study.
- Coach students on acting honorably in every day affairs.

Selections to Post in the Classroom
for Cultivating Conscience

Self command (Dotson & Dotson, 1997): Put a student figure on one side of the board and feet going across the width of the board. At the top, write "Step into tomorrow with..." and at the bottom, "Self command." On each of the feet going across the board, write techniques for self-control, such as "stop and think," "breathe deeply," "think before you react," "count to 10," "make wise food choices," and "consider the consequences."

Temperance (Dotson & Dotson, 1997): Put the heading "Control yourself or someone else will" on the top of a bulletin board and then display figures representing the principal's office, jail, hospital, police car, and parents looking angry.

Post an honor code (or more than one) that a student brings in, you find, or the class creates.

Sample Student Self-Monitoring
Cultivating Conscience

Encourage active learning by having students learn to monitor their own learning

Self Command
I know how to distract myself when I get impatient or frustrated.
I take charge of my own feelings and don't blame them on others.
I resist hurting someone when they leave themselves vulnerable.
I know what to do to relax myself when I get angry.
I know what to do to cheer myself up whn I get down.
I know how to communicate my needs without being aggressive.

Manage Influence and Power
I am respectful with the power that I have.
I share power with others.
I negotiate power respectfully.
I am aware that all sorts of messages bombard me daily.
I am aware that I am vulnerable to influence, whether I like it or not.
I reflect on how the media influence me.

Be Honorable
I admit my mistakes.
I tell the truth.
I keep promises.
I do not cheat.
I am honest about my achievements.
I don't take things that are not mine.
I remember to avoid pride.

Acting Responsibly

(Act Responsibly)

Ethical Motivation 3

WHAT

Acting responsibly might also be called conscientiousness. It is a desire to uphold all the possible ethical obligations one may have. Conscientiousness involves attending to the details of one's obligations, being a good steward of one's talents and wealth, and acting as a global citizen.

WHY

Conscientiousness is a compass for one's behavior that is influenced by one's obligations, sense of citizenship and stewardship. Conscientiousness also measures the current status of completing one's obligations.

SUBSKILLS OVERVIEW

Meet Obligations
Be a Good Steward
Be a Global Citizen

Web Wise

National Peace Corps Association: http://www.rpcv.org/pages/globalteachnet.cfm
An international assessment related to social studies is What Democracy Means to Ninth Graders: US Results from the International IEA Civic Education Study: http://nces.ed.gov/pubsearch
Institute for Global Communication has links to many other organizations (e.g., ConflictNet, EcoNet): www.igc.org
Links to web pages on government for kids: http://www.acf.hhs.gov/kids/

Acting Responsibly by Meeting Obligations

Creative and Expert Implementer Real-life Example

Nancy Reagan faithfully cared for her husband Ronald Reagan, who suffered from Alzheimer's disease. Because of her firm commitment to meeting the obligations of marriage vows she took many years ago, she remained faithful to him even as his ailment prevented him from recognizing her.

Ideas for Developing Skills

Level 1: Immersion in Examples and Opportunities
Attend to the big picture, Learn to recognize basic patterns

What is an obligation? Consider as a class the meaning of an "obligation." Who determines what they are? What are the consequences of not meeting them?

Finding obligations in the media (Dotson & Dotson, 1997). Use film and television clips to demonstrate different types of obligations that characters do and do not demonstrate.

Discuss obligations that parents have to their children (Dotson & Dotson, 1997). Spend time in class, in small groups or as a whole, discussing the obligations and responsibilities that parents have for their children. Do those obligations change with age?

Discuss obligations that children have to their parents and siblings (from Dotson & Dotson, 1997). Spend time in class, in a small group or as a whole, discussing the obligations that children have to their parents, and their siblings. How do they change with age? What will we owe our elderly parents?

Obligations concerning the environment. Bring in people representing different religious and cultural traditions to discuss their group's view on what obligations they have to the environment.

Responsibilities at work. Discuss with students how people demonstrate honesty within different areas of study (e.g., mathematics, biology) or work (e.g., police work, teaching, professional football) by (1) inviting a member of the profession to speak to the class on this topic; (2) finding examples in news and media; (3) having students interview a professional; (4) having students conduct research.

What is responsibility? According to Dominguez and Robin (1992), in *Your Money or Your Life*, responsibility is the "sense of how your life fits with your community and with the needs of the world" (p. 137). It means you are 'able' to 'respond,' which means you have choices about how to behave, and about what your limits are.

What are my duties?

Sir W. David Ross, a well-known philosopher who wrote, *The Right and the Good* (1939), lists the types of duties or obligatory actions that humans have:

- Keeping one's word
- Making amends
- Showing gratitude
- Fairness
- Improving the lives of others
- Not hurting others
- Self improvement in character
- Self improvement in intelligence

Starred activities within each subskill go together!

Acting Responsibly by Meeting Obligations

Ideas for Developing Skills

Level 1 (continued)

What is sustainability? Sustainability has to do with living in such a way that maintains the natural world for future generations and that allows all people a chance to live decently. According to Dominguez and Robin (1992), in *Your Money or Your Life*, a desire for sustainability comes from the understanding that humans rely on the natural world for all activities. (1) Have students investigate definitions and applications of sustainability. (2) Invite a speaker from a sustainability group (see www.sdgateway.net or http://www.webdirectory.com/Sustainable_Development/ for lists of organizations).

Level 2: Attention to Facts and Skills

Focus on detail and prototypical knowledge, Build knowledge

What kinds of obligations do people have? Have students interview their community elders (e.g., parents) about the obligations they have in general (as human beings) and in particular (as workers, parents, citizens). Put all the information gathered into a class chart.

Obligations to others. Have the class brainstorm a list of all of their obligations to others at home and at school. Are some more important than others? Do different people have different obligations? Why?

Mapping responsibilities. Students diagram all the responsibilities they have to others, including chores at home, taking care of pets, homework, etc. Have each student rate him or herself on their effectiveness at meeting these responsibilities.

Brainstorm responsibilities for homework. Brainstorm with the class ways to demonstrate responsibility for schoolwork. Have each student identify one area of responsibility they will work on.

Obligations associated with group membership (from Dotson & Dotson, 1997). Discuss what happens when a person doesn't meet their obligations. For example, (1) someone makes the entire group late for an event. (2) Someone doesn't follow through on finishing their part of a project. (3) Someone forgets to bring something important to a party. How do they feel about that person? Ask students to provide examples of when this has happened.

Starred 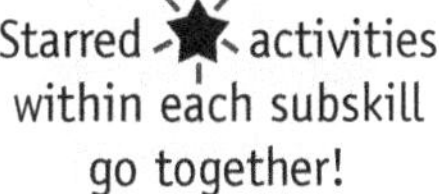 activities within each subskill go together!

Acting Responsibly by Meeting Obligations

Ideas for Developing Skills

Level 3: Practice Procedures
Set goals, Plan steps of problem solving, Practice skills

Fulfilling obligations. After identifying their responsibilities to others, students rate themselves on how well they are meeting their obligations. If they are having trouble, suggest ways to manage their obligations (e.g., keeping a calendar or notebook).

Identifying family/school obligations (Dotson & Dotson, 1997). Identify the obligations students have compared with other persons they live with, such as siblings. Does the baby of the family have the same responsibilities? Why or why not?

Organize school responsibilities. Give students time (perhaps weekly) to organize their notebooks, folders, and day planners in order to better facilitate meeting obligations. Take time to discuss and determine ways to maintain order of materials and responsibilities. **Assess** by reviewing each student's materials.

Consequences. Students write skits that teach a lesson about fulfilling one's moral obligation to another and act it out. The skit should include issues related to the repercussions for not following through with an obligation (e.g., a promise or helping someone). These can be presented to a school assembly or to a younger student classroom.

Level 4: Integrate Knowledge and Procedures
Execute plans, Solve problems

Take on a new responsibility. Encourage each student to take on a new responsibility at home, such as cooking dinner one night or taking care of a younger brother or sister or a neighbor's child for an hour. **Assess** by having them write a paragraph about their experience and the responsibilities involved and how taking responsibility makes them feel.

Guided social action. After determining what citizens are responsible for in their communities, have students identify an action that they should take within the community. Have the students devise a plan of action in collaboration with community members, making sure all obligations to all people are being considered. Then implement the plan, and evaluate the success of the implementation (for more details, see *Kids Guide to Social Action*, Lewis, Espelund, & Pernu, 1998). A critical feature is that the students need to feel ownership of the social action.

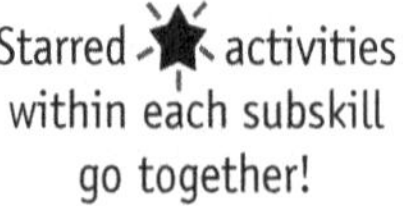

Starred activities within each subskill go together!

Assessment Hints

Meeting Obligations

Essays or Oral Reports. Have students write an essay or give an oral report about what they've learned about meeting obligations and who is a particularly good example of it in their lives.

Individual Performance. Following a cooperative or class activity targeting an issue related to meeting obligations, assess students on their individual contribution and performance.

Journaling. Over a period of time, perhaps a week, have students record the obligations that they have met, or have failed to meet, during the past week.

Checklist of Obligations. Have the students create a checklist of the obligations that they have in the various areas of their lives, i.e., family, home, school, friends, etc., and record their success at meeting them.

Acting Responsibly by Being a Good Steward

Paul Hawken is an environmentalist, business leader, lecturer, and best-selling author. He is one of the leading architects and advocates of reforming business practices so that they restore and not destroy the environment. In his own businesses he practices "capitalism as if living systems mattered." His work has transformed the hearts and minds of CEOs around the world towards a philosophy, and company policy, that is eco-friendly.

Creative and Expert Implementer Real-life Example

Ideas for Developing Skills

Level 1: Immersion in Examples and Opportunities

Attend to the big picture, Learn to recognize basic patterns

Examples of stewardship. Present students with examples of people (readings, video) who describe their stewardship and what they think about stewardship. Notice what motivates their stewardship and how they define it.

Examine local stewardship. How do local groups and traditions practice stewardship? Students interview representatives of local groups about this. **Assess** by writing up the interviews in report from.

Limits of resources. Discuss the limits of all resources (ecological, social capital, personal energy, time—hours in the day) and how people are always making choices (usually not consciously).

History of stewardship. How have groups practiced stewardship? Have your students break up into groups and choose and present on a particular group that has shown stewardship (e.g., the Sierra Club, the World Wildlife Fund, etc.). **Assess** with group presentations.

Stewardship at work. Discuss with students how people demonstrate honesty within different areas of study (e.g., mathematics, biology) or work (e.g., police work, teaching, professional football) by (1) inviting a member of the profession to speak to the class on this topic; (2) finding examples in news and media; (3) having students interview a professional; (4) having students conduct research.

What is property? Discuss the Western notion of property. (a) Private Property: What can be owned? Who owns what? What do people do with what they own? Can they do anything they want with their own property? Point out that in owning property, one feels more invested in it and concerned for its welfare. (b) Public Property: Why are some things considered public property? What does that mean? What obligations do we each have for public property and why?

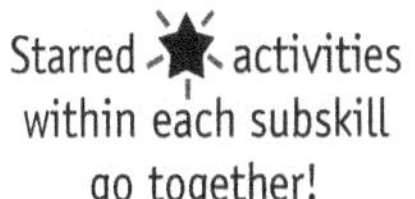
Starred activities within each subskill go together!

Acting Responsibly by Being a Good Steward

Ideas for Developing Skills

Level 2: Attention to Facts and Skills

Focus on detail and prototypical knowledge, Build knowledge

Brainstorming exercise on stewardship. After defining what stewardship is, have the students brainstorm about different ways that they themselves have shown good stewardship. How have people whom they know shown good stewardship?

Assessing resource availability. Find examples of ways that people budget their resource use. What are some effective ways that the students budget their own resources?

Create a poster demonstrating stewardship. Have students work in groups to create posters demonstrating stewardship. **Assess** by observing participation and quality of the poster.

Pursuing good health as stewardship. Brainstorm with the class about how caring for one's body, appearance, and overall good health are related to good stewardship. What are some of the benefits that one might experience from such pursuits?

Discussion of respecting other people's property (Dotson & Dotson, 1997). Ask students what it means to respect other people's property. How do they feel when someone messes with their stuff?

Level 3: Practice Procedures

Set goals, Plan steps of problem solving, Practice skills

Write letters of thanks to those who show good stewardship locally. Have the students write letters to the local groups and clubs that have shown admirable stewardship in their group's activities. Include in the letter the ways in which the group's stewardship has helped the class and the community.

Planning stewardship. After finding out about their own stewardship (based on above Level 2 activity "Brainstorming exercise on stewardship"), students make a plan for improvement. Assess with write-up of self-assessment and improvement plan.

Self-assessment on resource use. Students keep a record of how much of the following they use in one week: water, heat, electricity, foods, transportation, etc. Students come together and graph their usage of each resource.

Advantages of being good stewards (Dotson & Dotson, 1997). Ask students to identify the advantages of being good stewards. How do they and others benefit?

Starred activities within each subskill go together!

Acting Responsibly by Being a Good Steward

Ideas for Developing Skills

Level 3 (continued)

Creating plans for respecting property. Students create a plan together for respecting school property. Whether it be through a poster campaign, or patrolling, or "town-meetings," the class should lay out a detailed plan to implement their objectives.

Invite a local expert. Have the students invite and host a local expert(s) on stewardship in a particular domain, e.g., energy conservation expert, recycling commissioner, etc. Ask the local expert to help the class develop a plan for stewardship (for the class, the school, personally). Invite the expert back in several months to hear reports about how the plan implementation has progressed.

Self-assessment. (1) Students interview community members or elders with questions listed below. (2) Students answer the questions themselves. Sample questions: (a) How are you a good steward of your gifts and talents? (b) How well do you take care of yourself physically, mentally/emotionally, spiritually? (c) How are you a good steward of our land? The earth? (d) How are you a good steward of the place you work or go to school? (e) How are you a good steward of the place you live? (3) Make plans to be a good steward and carry them out.

Stewardship in a particular domain. Invite a representative from a particular line of work (e.g., farming, manufacturing, labor, management, social service) and ask them questions like these (send the questions ahead of time): (a) How is your business or line of work a good steward of our land, of our people, of our planet? (b) What steps do you take to maintain a healthy planet, a healthy neighborhood?

Level 4: Integrate Knowledge and Procedures

Execute plans, Solve problems

Resource budgeting. Using information from their self assessment (developed in above Level 3 activity "Self-assessment") on resource usage, have students budget themselves on resources usage. The class or group can decide together on limits. **Assess** by having students keep track for a week and report to their group and class.

Implement an action plan for a healthy lifestyle. Have the students create an exhaustive action plan for good health. Include things such as diet, exercise, appearance, time management, etc. Ask them to implement their action plan for one week and report back to the class about their success and the benefits of it.

Acting Responsibly by Being a Good Steward

Ideas for Developing Skills

Level 4 (continued)

Group stewardship of the environment. Students participate in a local group that advocates environmental stewardship (e.g., recycling, roadside clean-up, etc). Consider participating in the "Care for a Highway" program where a club or organization agrees to keep a stretch of highway clean for a period of time.

I respect property. Students implement the plan a plan for respecting school property in the Level 3 activity "Creating plans for respecting property." Whether it be through a poster campaign, or patrolling, or "town-meetings," the class should implement the detailed plan for the benefit of the entire school community. Assess with a report on implemented plan.

Assessment Hints

Be a Good Steward

Essays or Oral Reports. Have students write an essay or give an oral report about what they've learned about stewardship and who is a particularly good example of it in their lives.

Interview. Assess an interview by having the students report back to the class, either in a written report or orally, what they talked about and learned from the interview.

Journaling. Over a period of time, perhaps a week, have students record the obligations that they have, or have failed to meet, during the past week.

Write a Letter. Have the students write a letter to express concern to the White House, the Congress, an environmental group, etc., about an issue of importance to them regarding stewardship.

Group Presentations. Have the students break up into small groups to create a presentation for the class on particular groups that support stewardship.

Posters/Graphs. Assess by having the students, individually or in small groups, create a poster representing that which they've learned about having regard for creation.

Acting Responsibly by Being a Global Citizen

Creative and Expert Implementer Real-life Example

George J. Mitchell, a former U.S. Senator from Maine (1980-1995), and Senate Majority Leader from 1989-1995, represented the U.S. in peace talks in various parts of the world beginning in the 1990s. He is particularly noted for negotiating the 1998 peace accord for power sharing in Northern Ireland.

Ideas for Developing Skills

Level 1: Immersion in Examples and Opportunities

Attend to the big picture, Learn to recognize basic patterns

Documents of global significance. Have students read one or more of the following documents: United Nations Declaration of Human Rights; United Nations Declaration of the Rights of the Child; Kyoto Global Warming agreement; Nuclear Arms Test Ban Treaty. Have them gather more information from the web or library and report on it. If possible, invite experts into class to answer questions about the document and its impact.

Understanding national citizenship around the world. Conduct research on citizenship in other countries (selected by student or teacher). Report on similarities and differences with U.S. citizenship. Discuss why it might be important to understand the differences in various nations' understanding of citizenship.

Consider the "global thinkers" in your life. Have each student make a list of the "global thinkers" in their lives. (Global thinkers are people who think about being a global citizen, who are concerned for people who live in other countries or for future generations, and who think about their impact on the future of the world.) In what ways are they global thinkers? How do they stretch us to see the world, and our relationship to it, in a different way? What other qualities do they have? **Assess** by having the students report on the best global thinker he or she knows.

Level 2: Attention to Facts and Skills

Focus on detail and prototypical knowledge, Build knowledge

Historical examples of global citizenship. Ask the students to brainstorm about those in history who might be considered global citizens and why. Consider those who have impacted the world for good, such as inventors, peacemakers, religious leaders, etc.

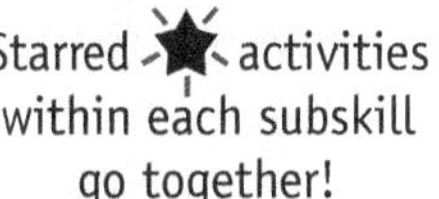
Starred activities within each subskill go together!

Acting Responsibly by Being a Global Citizens

Ideas for Developing Skills

Level 2 (continued)

Current examples of global citizens. Ask students to (a) define what they think global citizenship means, (b) explain the behavior of one who might be described as a global citizen, (c) what might the students do to be better global citizens?

Highlight global citizens. Share with the class how people like Jimmy Carter and Mother Teresa of Calcutta have been, through their work and their lives, global citizens. (You can find stories about such people in numerous books at your library.)

Ethical role model. Students are encouraged to be in contact with an ethical role model who is generous to others on a regular basis. Optimally, this ethical role model would be similar in many respects to the students (age, gender), yet have higher status (is considered "cool") and perform actions in situations that are similar to the ones the students face. **Assess** by having students write up their interviews and present them to the class.

What can you do at school? Brainstorm a list of ways in which the students could demonstrate global citizenship at school. Point out that global citizenship can be exercised right at home and that things we do everyday (e.g., recycle, be informed about world conflicts, write our government representatives, etc.) can potentially effect the wider world community. **Assess** by having students compose a personal list of ways they are already good global citizens.

Level 3: Practice Procedures

Set goals, Plan steps of problem solving, Practice skills

World awareness activities. Build awareness of world problems with activities such as "Hunger: A World View" (Center for Learning, 1997) an activities-based lesson about world hunger meant to raise awareness about the problem of world hunger and how one can help. The class should follow through with one of the ideas and help. **Assess** by having students choose an activity and write up how they could tackle it.

Invite international organizations that have a global impact. Invite someone from an international organization such as the United Way, the Red Cross, the International Monetary Fund, or another such organization to speak to the class about what they do and how they are funded. Ask the speaker to talk about the importance of their work and the impact it has on the people they serve. **Assess** with reports on what they heard and how they could help.

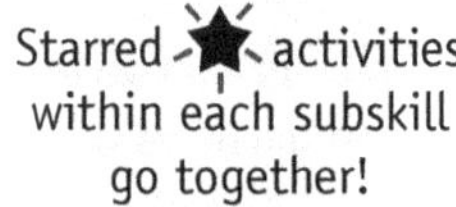
Starred activities within each subskill go together!

Acting Responsibly by Being a Global Citizens

Ideas for Developing Skills

Level 3 (continued)

Investigate an international organization. Identify an international organization that provides services throughout the world and write a report on this group. What goods or services does it provide? Where does it get funding? For whom might such an organization be particularly important? **Assess** with report.

Self-assessment. Policy experts have identified the public virtues and values that a global citizen should have in the 21st century. It is anticipated that if people around the world do not develop these characteristics, there will be more wars and threats of war. The experts agreed on the following characteristics, in descending order of importance.

1. Approaches problems as member of a global society
2. Works cooperatively with others and takes responsibility for one's roles and responsibilities in society
3. Understands, accepts, and tolerates cultural differences
4. Thinks in a critical and systematic way
5. Resolves conflict in a non-violent manner
6. Adopts a way of life that protects the environment
7. Respects and defends human rights
8. Participates in public life at all levels of civic discourse
9. Makes full use of information-based technologies

(1) Have students interview community leaders about these characteristics: do they think they are important? Do they see them in the citizenry? How are they promoting them? (2) Find examples of other communities success at fostering these characteristics. (3) How can the class and school foster these characteristics?

Being a global citizen at work. Have students interview adults from different professions and lines of work about the list of citizenship characteristics. Do they follow these recommendations? Why or why not? Have students report on their findings.

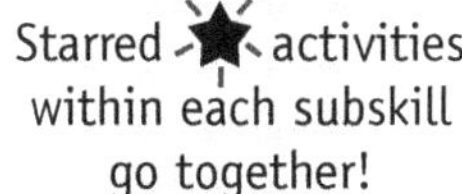
Starred activities
within each subskill
go together!

Acting Responsibly by Being a Global Citizens

Ideas for Developing Skills

Level 4: Integrate Knowledge and Procedures

Execute plans, Solve problems

Adopt a child/family (Dotson & Dotson, 1997). Ask your students if they would like to adopt a child in another country. Figure out what it would cost to do this and make sure that your students are willing to bring in the money. Have the students write a letter to the child. Alternatively, you could ask the students to adopt a needy family for the holiday. Have the class talk about what they want to provide for that family and divide up the responsibilities. (You might wish to make sure that the needy family does not have children at your school.)

Be a global citizen! Choose a way to exercise global citizenship and do it! Whether it be something that the student does regularly, or something that they've taken on anew, at the end of a week have the students report to the class on what they've done (e.g., recycling, study of global conflicts/issues, wrote letters to government representatives about issues of concern).

Voluntary simplicity for a day. Have students read about voluntary simplicity or invite to class a local community member who voluntarily lives simply. Ask them to describe what this means. Have each student identify one area where he or she can simplify his or her life. Have them practice simplifying for a period of time, and report on their progress.

Assessment Hints

Global Citizenship

Essays or Oral Reports. Have students write an essay or give an oral report about what they've learned about global citizenship and who is a particularly good example of it in their lives.

Interview. Assess an interview by having the students report back to the class, either in a written report or orally, what they talked about and learned from the interview.

Checklist of Global Citizenry. Have the students create a checklist of the things that one must do to be a good global citizen.

Group Presentations. Have the students break up into small groups and present to the class on a global issue, i.e., world hunger, arms proliferation, etc.

Starred activities within each subskill go together!

Create a Climate
to Develop Responsibility

- Write or review class rules and discuss each student's responsibility to abide by these rules.
- On a daily basis, emphasize the importance of fulfilling one's ethical obligations (e.g., keeping your word).
- Set clear goals and responsibilities for ethical behaviors and attitudes.
- Discuss global citizenship regularly.
- Model and explain good citizenship.

Selections to Post in the Classroom
for Developing Responsibility

(Dotson & Dotson, 1997)

Dedicate a bulletin board to "Responsible Students of the Week." Spotlight two or three responsible students a week by putting their photos on the board in order to highlight and reinforce the behavior.

Put a very large picture of a dollar bill on the board. Add the words, "Stretch yourself... Give generously!"

Acting Responsibly

Encourage active learning by having students learn to monitor their own learning

Meet Obligations

Situation Specific

I think about my responsibilities to others in this situation.
I think about the effects that I can have on others.
I know what responsibilities I have in this situation.
In this situation I did what I said I was going to do.
I did my work in a timely fashion.
I did my best.
I completed all my responsibilities.

General

When I make a promise, I keep it.
I am punctual.
I do my chores at home.
I don't make excuses to get out of responsibilities.
I can be counted on.
I try as hard as I can.

Be a Good Steward

When I use a resource, I am careful not to waste it.

Be a Global Citizen

I am concerned about the welfare of others in other countries.
I think about how my actions affect people in other countries.

Being a Community Member
(Help Others)

WHAT
Helping others is a concrete way to show ethical motivation and requires skills of cooperation and acting thoughtfully. Ways to help include sharing one's resources and being of service to meet needs in the community.

WHY
In order to be helpful, one must notice the opportunity and one must know appropriate ways to help. Without the awareness of opportunity and appropriate action, individuals will find it difficult to share and be of service to others.

SUBSKILLS OVERVIEW
Cooperate
Act Thoughtfully
Share Resources
- Generosity
- Choosing Service

Web Wise
Test students on group skills at http://www.bolton.ac.uk/lskills/TLTP3/entersite.html

Being a Community Member by Cooperating

Creative and Expert Implementer Real-life Example

Habitat for Humanity, International, an organization founded by ***Millard*** and ***Linda Fuller***, brings together people around the world who cooperate in building houses with and for those who could not otherwise afford a home. Those who build the houses are ordinary citizens who often learn on the job.

Ideas for Developing Skills

Level 1: Immersion in Examples and Opportunities

Attend to the big picture, Learn to recognize basic patterns

Cooperation at school. Invite a school official or superintendent to discuss the importance of cooperation at school. What does it look like? What benefit is there for the class when each individual cooperates?

Cooperation in public places. Invite a local politician or police officer to discuss the importance of cooperation in public places (e.g., train stations, airports, grocery stores, ticket lines, parks, etc.). How do we benefit as individuals, as a society, from cooperation?

Cooperation at home. Students interview family members about the importance of cooperation in the home. Ask students for examples from their families of how cooperation is needed. What are some of the benefits of cooperating in a family?

Cooperating at work. Discuss with students how people cooperate with each other within different areas of study (e.g., mathematics, biology) or work (e.g., police work, teaching, professional football) by (1) inviting a member of the profession to speak to the class on this topic; (2) finding examples in news and media; (3) having students interview a professional; (4) having students conduct research.

Interview on cooperation on the job. Have students interview an adult about cooperation on the job. What situations require cooperation in the business world? In a factory or hospital setting how does health and safety depend on cooperation?

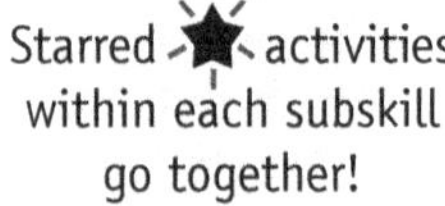
Starred activities within each subskill go together!

Observing cooperation on TV (Dotson & Dotson, 1997). Ask students to watch their favorite TV program to find examples of cooperation or non-cooperation and the consequences.

Being a Community Member by Cooperating

Ideas for Developing Skills

Level 2: Attention to Facts and Skills

Focus on detail and prototypical knowledge, Build knowledge

Teach cooperation skills. Teach the class fundamentals of team dynamics, such as choosing a team leader, writing team rules, and encouraging discussion from all members. **Assess** by reports of ways in which cooperation is important.

Age group differences in cooperating skills. Bring in a community member who works successfully with people of different ages. Ask the person what kinds of skills are needed to work with each group. Students reflect on the skills needed for working with different age groups.

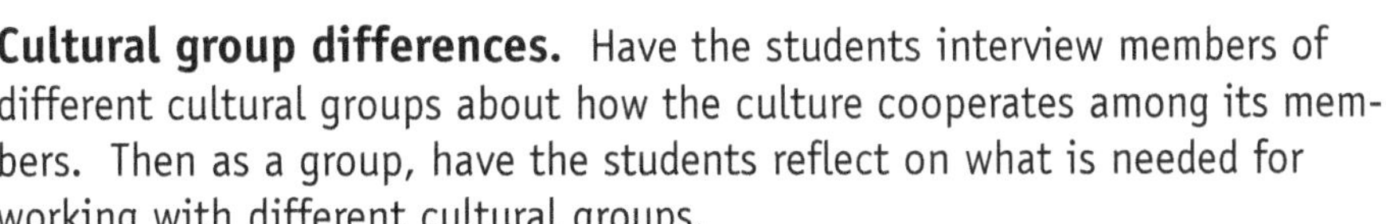

Cultural group differences. Have the students interview members of different cultural groups about how the culture cooperates among its members. Then as a group, have the students reflect on what is needed for working with different cultural groups.

Brainstorm attitudes for effective teamwork (Dotson & Dotson, 1997). Brainstorm and create a list of attitudes needed to work effectively on a team, such as accepting suggestions, being friendly, compromising, and not being bossy.

Discuss importance of every member of group (Dotson & Dotson, 1997). Discuss the concept that "None of us is as smart as all of us." Is this true? Ask for examples of how cooperative effort has resulted in great discoveries. Assess by having students list the things that they bring to a group that others might not.

Global cooperation (Dotson & Dotson, 1997). Introduce the concept of cooperation on a global scale with a discussion of the United Nations. Bring this concept down to the level of local government, perhaps by discussing an issue of local relevance in which parties are divided on the best decision.

EM-4 Being a Community Member

Level 3: Practice Procedures

Set goals, Plan steps of problem solving, Practice skills

Role play cooperative skills. Students act out cooperative behaviors in different situations and with different groups.

Practice cooperation skills. Drawing on a conversation about team dynamics, practice the principles by writing classroom rules.

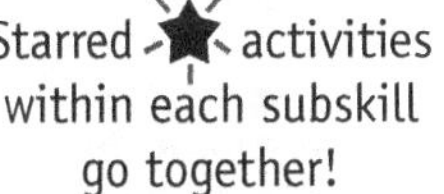
Starred activities
within each subskill
go together!

Being a Community Member by Cooperating

Ideas for Developing Skills

Level 3 (continued)

Practice age group differences in cooperating skills. After bringing in a community member who works successfully with people of different ages, ask the person what kinds of skills are needed to work with each group. Encourage the students to consciously practice these skills at home and at school for a week and report back to class about the effects of their cooperating.

Brief cooperative project (Dotson & Dotson, 1997). Give students a small cooperative project that can be completed in a short time period. At the end of the time allotted, discuss any problems that occurred when working together. Did one or two members take over the project? How were differences handled?

Group poster project (Dotson & Dotson, 1997). Have students work in small groups to develop a poster about character education at your school. Allow the students to be as creative as they want using the materials you provide. As the groups are working, walk around providing instruction on how to make decisions and resolve differences as a team. Assess by observation and poster. Post posters in classroom.

Practice cultural cooperation. After interviewing members of different cultural groups about how his or her culture cooperates among its members, have the students practice these skills in the classroom. Encourage them to reflect in conversation about their observations.

Level 4: Integrate Knowledge and Procedures

Execute plans, Solve problems

Cooperative group activities. Students learn about the different ways that groups can work and the different roles that group members can take. Students then form small groups and are given a complex problem (could be social or logic problem) that is not easily solved. The groups then have to discuss what roles the group members are going to have and how they are going to solve the problem. **Assess** by having the student write a self-report and/or a group report analyzing the role play. Have them address how well they worked together and how they benefited from cooperating.

Long-term group project (Dotson & Dotson, 1997). Give students a more complex assignment to complete, such as writing a group story or doing a group research project. Encourage students to divide the task into sections and have each person responsible for a certain section.

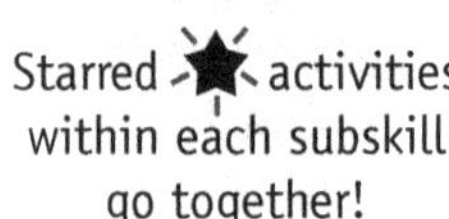
Starred activities
within each subskill
go together!

Being a Community Member by Cooperating

Ideas for Developing Skills

Level 4 (continued)

Group skits (Dotson & Dotson, 1997). Have students work together in small groups to write skits about the school year, summer vacation, etc. Provide a period of time each day to work on the skits, and have the groups perform for the school or for younger children.

Assessment Hints

Cooperate

Essays or Oral Reports. Have students write an essay or give an oral report about what they've learned about cooperation and who is a particularly good example of it in their lives.

Interview. Assess an interview by having the students report back to the class, either in a written report or orally, what they talked about and learned from the interview..

Individual Performance. Following a cooperative or class activity targeting an issue related to cooperation, assess students on their individual contribution and performance.

List of Examples. Assess by having the students, individually or in small groups, create a list of examples of cooperation or non-cooperation from television or movies.

Role Plays. Have the students write a skit and act out the roles of the characters demonstrating what they've discussed and learned about cooperation.

Posters. Assess by having the students, individually or in small groups, create a poster representing that which they've learned about cooperation.

Ideas to Post for Developing Responsibility

- Cover the board with pictures of groups of people working together on projects. Use the header, "Cooperation gets things done!"

- Show a globe and cut-outs representing people from around the world. Link the people-figures around the outside of the world. Use the header, "Cooperation: Key to a Global Community."

- Ask the students to help create a collage with images from magazines and newspapers which represent the things for which the students are most thankful. Put a heading on the board such as "The things for which we are thankful" or perhaps, simply, "Thankfulness."

Creative and Expert Implementer Real-life Example

Being a Community Member by Acting Thoughtfully

Arthur Ashe grew up in a segregated neighborhood but after he picked up a tennis racket he broke into the historically white game of tennis, winning many championships. He was the first African American to be ranked number one tennis player in the world. When he was undergoing heart surgery in the early 1980s, he contracted the HIV-AIDS virus from a blood transfusion. He spent the last years of his life raising awareness of AIDS to a level where the overriding reaction was no longer paranoia.

Ideas for Developing Skills

Level 1: Immersion in Examples and Opportunities
Attend to the big picture, Learn to recognize basic patterns

Thoughtful role models. Have students investigate instances of acting thoughtfully. Some people do it all the time. Students could investigate: (1) celebrities, (2) officials, (3) historical people, (4) community members, and (5) people they know. Have students identify how these people acted thoughtfully.

Thoughtfulness in fields of study and at work. Study a particular field and those who work in it. Find examples of thoughtful action. Have students identify and describe how actions were thoughtful.

Level 2: Attention to Facts and Skills
Focus on detail and prototypical examples, Build knowledge

Thoughtfully acknowledging others. (1) Have students pay attention to how others acknowledge them throughout the day (e.g., a person on the street, the clerk at the store, teachers they don't know, custodians, friends, family members, etc.), writing down each encounter and how the other person reacted to them when they first met. (2) Have students interview their families about how they acknowledge other people and how the family members expect to be acknowledged by others (e.g., a stranger on the street makes eye contact and says hello).

Acting thoughtfully environmentally. Discuss how one's behavior towards the environment affects the welfare of others. (You might discuss whether "others" should include animals and plants.) For example, things you leave behind: like litter on the floor, in the hall, in the street; dirt or poisons you leave behind: in the class, in the bathroom, in a public place, on the lawn or in the sewer/ground water; things you have taken: like plants, rocks from a protected park, a captured animal; overuse of water depleting the ground water supply. Discuss ways to remember to be thoughtful and think of others.

Being a Community Member by Acting Thoughtfully
Ideas for Developing Skills
Level 2 (continued)

Thoughtful minding of your body (Forni, 2002). With younger students, discuss with students that the way one manages one's body when with others demonstrates one's attitude towards courtesy. Discuss grooming habits to remember (e.g., clean and odor free body, washed hair, clean nails, face, neck, teeth, makeup applied well, breath, clean and unrumpled clothing in good condition). Discuss the importance of grooming in private (nails, scratching, combing) including keeping fingers away from mouth, ears, nose. Discuss mouth etiquette: keep mouth closed when chewing; not making noises with mouth; covering mouth when coughing sneezing; not snorting or spitting. Have students make posters to remind others in the school of how to be courteous with one's body.

Acting thoughtfully with global awareness. Discuss how the activities in one part of the globe can affect the people in another part of the globe (e.g., dust storms in Africa cause hurricanes in the eastern seaboard). Discuss how people's actions can also have effects big and small (e.g., Chernobyl disaster fallout killing reindeer in Lapland; buying mahogany or ivory encourages poachers of these materials in other countries). Have students find examples of actions and global effects.

Acting thoughtfully in civic discourse. Discuss the importance of civil dialogue in a democracy. If the government is of the people, then all people should have a say and ideas should be discussed. Practice civil dialogue in class. Use role plays of specific scenarios.

Acting thoughtfully using technology. Discuss the importance of treating others thoughtfully when using the internet, email, and other forms of technological communication. Have students find examples of respectful communication.

Helping others (Gibbs, Potter, & Goldstein, 1995). Have students practice these steps to simple helping (thinking aloud for the inner dialogue). (1) Is there a need? Does the person need help? Does the person need or want my help? (2) Think of different ways you could be helpful. Can you do something for the person or should you get help from someone else? (3) Plan ahead. Decide whether you should help now or later. (4) Offer your help. Don't feel bad if the person says no. Examples of situations to role play: (a) A teacher has lots of boxes to move. (b) Your friend lost their wallet or purse. (c) An adult slips on the sidewalk and drops their bag of groceries, which fall out. (d) Two of your friends get into an argument and get so upset they are about to harm each other.

Being a Community Member by Acting Thoughtfully

Ideas for Developing Skills

Level 3: Practice Procedures

Set goals, Plan steps of problem solving, Practice skills

Being thoughtful of others' time (Forni, 2002). After discussing respecting others' time, ask students to keep a journal of observations about time and report after a set period of time. In order to respect other people's time, you must value it as you value your own (although sometimes there are people who don't value their own time). How to show respect for others' time: (a) Be punctual: call if you'll be more than 5 minutes late. (b) Wait your turn and don't take advantage of it. (c) Take into consideration what is a good time to phone someone according to their perceptions. (d) Don't make people wait for you. (e) Don't put people on call waiting unless it's urgent. Have students practice and keep track of their (and their friend's or partner's) behaviors. Expect all students to be respectful of others' time during school.

Thoughtfully respecting others' space (Forni, 2002). After discussing respecting space, ask students to keep a journal of observations about space and report after a set period of time. Treating other people's space and bodies the way they want them to be treated is a fundamental aspect of being considerate. There are large cultural differences in this, so pay attention to your companion's comfort level and be flexible in how you respond to them. (a) Pay attention to the space between you and the person you are talking with. Note the comfort level of the other person when you are talking with them—if they step back, don't step forward. Let the other person guide you in figuring out what makes them comfortable. (b) Touch people only if they want to be touched and only in public body spaces (i.e., hands, arms, shoulders). (c) Observe and respect personal territory. For example, don't touch other people's things or go into their rooms without permission. (d) Respect the privacy of other people's communications (e.g., emails, notes, letters, grades).

Speaking kindly (Forni, 2002). Discuss the importance of speaking kindly to others: Remember that words have power. Be aware that when you speak to another, you are interacting with a vulnerable human being. Keep the welfare of the other person in mind when you speak. Look at Forni's rules for speaking kindly. Have students practice these behaviors in class and expect these behaviors of them.

Being a Community Member by Acting Thoughtfully

Ideas for Developing Skills

Level 3 (continued)

Avoiding speaking unkindly of someone to others (Forni, 2002). (a) Discuss how we are all tempted to speak (or email) unkindly about someone when we are feeling insecure about our self worth, when we are envious of someone's achievement, when we want revenge against the person, or when we think it raises our standing in the group or makes us closer to the listener. (b) Discuss what damage can be done if we do speak unkindly of someone to others. For example, they can feel hurt if they find out, their reputation can be damaged, our own reputation may be damaged, it is cowardly because the other person cannot defend him/herself, we can offend the listeners, our words can prompt another to harm that person or the group the person belongs to. (c) Discuss what you can do if someone does say bad things in your presence about others. For example, you can leave, you can be silent if it is short-lived and mild, you can say something positive about the person, you can tell the attacker that you are uncomfortable and don't want to discuss this. (d) Have students brainstorm about what kinds of gossip go around about others. Brainstorm about what a person could say to the speaker. Select a few to role play in which the listener says (assertively) that they don't want to hear it.

Accept and give praise (Forni, 2002). Have students practice giving sincere compliments. Tell them that by giving sincere praise we help others become aware of their gifts. "Through our praise we reveal to people who they are" (p. 70). The more we give praise the less we feel vulnerable about doing it. Remind them that small compliments are fine. Students can use terms like:

I appreciate the way you...
Thanks for working so hard when...
One of the things I enjoy most about you is....
Our class couldn't be successful without your...
You did a great job of....
What a good idea!
Thanks for....
Have students practice receiving compliments, too, by saying "thank you" without having to reciprocate hastily.

Respect others' opinions (Forni, 2002). Respecting the opinion of others means that we understand that people are entitled to opinions different from our own and that we don't present our own opinions as the truth. If you criticize someone's opinion, they may feel rejected and so it is important to learn how to disagree politely by (a) finding some part of the opinion that you agree with and build from there, (b) indicating that the opinion is not unreasonable, (c) saying that if you knew more you might agree, and (d) being generous in your reaction. Have students practice different ways of politely disagreeing with each other. Give them role plays and have them demonstrate each type of disagreement.

Being a Community Member by Acting Thoughtfully

Ideas for Developing Skills

Level 3 (continued)

Be agreeable (Forni, 2002). Being agreeable in conversation you must be able to consider that you might be wrong and to admit that you don't know. You need to train yourself to do these things. You also need to train yourself to see the similarities between your own views and the views of others. You also need to practice receiving civil gestures from others that you don't think you need but which make the relationship go smoothly (like someone lending you a pencil because they think you don't have a good one). Have students role play situations where students have different opinions about (a) what movie to see (b) what activity to engage in on the weekend, etc.

Level 4: Integrate Knowledge and Procedures

Execute plans, Solve problems

Mentor a younger child in acting thoughtfully. Have students develop several lessons on acting thoughtfully for younger children. Have them work with a younger child on building these skills.

Shadow an adult who acts thoughtfully. Have students shadow an adult who is skilled at acting thoughtfully and write in a journal about it. Have students imitate the thoughtful acts and report on it.

Assessment Hints

Act thoughtfully

Reflective activities. Students reflect on personal experience and personal skill development such as essays, keeping a report diary.

Creative work. To inspire others to be thoughtful, students create poems, songs, music, plays, visual art.

Knowledge tests. Quiz students about the elements of showing thoughtfulness in different situations, domains and cultures.

Interview. Assess an interview by having the students report back to the class, either in a written report or orally, about what they talked about and learned from the interview.

List of Exemplars. Assess by having the students, individually or in small groups, create a list of those who have demonstrated impressive thoughtful actions, whether in their lives or from the wider culture.

Being a Community Member by Sharing Resources

Creative and Expert Implementer Real-life Example

Bill and Melinda Gates have begun a charitable multi-billion dollar foundation that gives away millions of dollars a year to those in need, particularly in the areas of health care and immunization in economically poor nations.

Ideas for Developing Skills

Level 1: Immersion in Examples and Opportunities

Attend to the big picture, Learn to recognize basic patterns

Stories about helping. (1) Discuss stories that articulate a message about the impact a person can have on another. The students should consider the value of helping others, and how valuing others can lead to a sense of ethical obligation to help others. Address specific questions like: Is it wrong not to help another person when you can? What if everyone thought that someone else would help the person in need? Students can also discuss what actions in the story were obliged and which weren't and why. You may find specific stories at http://www.uensd.org/usoe_pages/ic/chared/anecdotal.html, such as "Climbing Mt. Fuji" (about unity, reaching a common goal), "Lord Baden-Powell" (about concern for others' welfare and what one person can do). (2) *The Struggle to Survive* (Center for Learning, 1994) is a narrative about two boys struggling to survive on their own. The story is meant to develop "an awareness of the value of caring for and helping others."

Interview someone who shares resources well. Have the students determine someone whom they know well who shares their resources (e.g., possessions, time, money) and interview them. Whether it be a parent, grandparent or even peer, have them question them about their motivations and what benefit they themselves get from sharing.

Resources that can be shared. Students identify resources people can share (from possessions, money, to time and support). Break the class into groups and have each of the groups take up the different sorts of resources that can be shared by a person, a family, a nation, a church community, etc. Assess presentations to the class by each group.

Sharing with others at work. Discuss with students how people share with each other within different areas of study (e.g., mathematics, biology) or work (e.g., police work, teaching, professional football) by (1) inviting a member of the profession to speak to the class on this topic; (2) finding examples in news and media; (3) having students interview a professional; (4) having students conduct research.

Starred activities within each subskill go together!

Being a Community Member by Sharing Resources

Ideas for Developing Skills

Level 1 (continued)

Interview someone who does service. Have the students interview people involved in service activities. Have them inquire about their experiences. What compels them to do service? How do they benefit from doing service?

Highlight generous people (Dotson & Dotson, 1997). Share with the class how people like Booker T. Washington and Mother Teresa of Calcutta have contributed generously to the lives of others. (You can find stories about such people in numerous books at your library.) **Assess** with report.

Consider the generous people in your life. Have each student make a list of the most generous people in their lives. In what ways are they generous? How do they feel about those people? What other qualities do they have? Assess by having the students report on the most generous person he or she knows.

Level 2: Attention to Facts and Skills

Focus on detail and prototypical knowledge, Build knowledge

Resources that can be shared. Students research and identify resources people can share (from possessions, money, to time and support). Break the class into groups and have each of the groups take up the different sorts of resources that can be shared by a person, a family, a nation, a church community, etc.

Why people choose to share their resources. Facilitate a class discussion which asks the question why people, families, nations, churches might choose to share their resources.

Interview someone who shares resources well. Have the students determine someone whom they know to share well their resources and interview them. Whether it be a parent, grandparent or even peer, have them question them about their motivations and what benefit they themselves get from sharing.

Brainstorm about things we can do to be generous (Dotson & Dotson, 1997). Brainstorm with the class the small ways they can be generous with their time and energy. For example, a student might choose to give up a 20-minute free period to volunteer in the school office or with younger students. **Assess** according to feasibility of plan made.

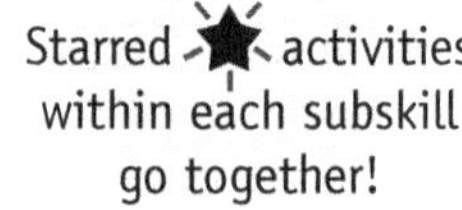
Starred activities within each subskill go together!

Being a Community Member by Sharing Resources

Ideas for Developing Skills

Level 2 (continued)

Ethical role model. Students are encouraged to be in contact with an ethical role model who is generous to others on a regular basis. Optimally, this ethical role model would be similar in many respects to the students (age, gender), yet have higher status (is considered "cool") and perform actions in situations that are similar to the one's the students face. **Assess** by having students write up their interviews and present them to the class.

Blood Drive Information Day (Dotson & Dotson, 1997). Invite a person from the Red Cross to speak to your class about blood drives and organ donation. Why are these functions important? Discuss generosity in this context.

What can you do at school (Dotson & Dotson, 1997)? Brainstorm a list of ways in which the students could do something generous for their school. Point out that generosity can be a gift of time, talent and treasure. **Assess** by having students compose a personal list of ways they are already being generous.

Create an exhaustive list of community service providers. Use the internet, the phone book, municipal government information, church bulletins, etc. to create as complete a list as possible of the service opportunities in your community. Include contact information for those who are interested in getting involved and share with your school.

Learning about service learning. Students find out about service learning in their school and community. What options are available to people who are interested in service learning? What learning might be involved in service? How might it be best accomplished?

Investigate a charitable organization. Identify a charitable organization that depends on volunteers to stay in business and write a report on this group. What goods or services does it provide others? What does it ask of its volunteers? What do the volunteers do? What do the volunteers gain from the experience? **Assess** with report.

Discuss volunteer service. What are some of the opportunities for service in our society? Who does service? Who benefits from volunteer service? What are some of the benefits that the volunteer receives?

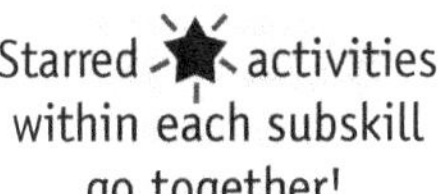

Starred activities within each subskill go together!

Being a Community Member by Sharing Resources

Ideas for Developing Skills

Level 3: Practice Procedures

Set goals, Plan steps of problem solving, Practice skills

Sharing *my* resources. Have students identify their own personal resources and ways that they can share them with others. Brainstorm about how one can share resources while maintaining the dignity of the other person, particularly persons in need.

Create a plan for sharing resources. Students identify a resource they want to share in a particular situation or with a particular person or group. Students create a plan for sharing it over a period of time. **Assess** by having students write-up their detailed plan.

Perspective taking. Students find ethical situations in stories about sharing with others in need. Students can either elaborate on the text by writing a continuation or tangent to the story (related to helping behavior) or present the story to the class, or group, by acting out one or more roles of the characters involved in a sequence related to helping others.

World awareness activities. Build awareness of world problems with activities such as "Hunger: A World View" (Center for Learning, 1997) an activities-based lesson about world hunger meant to raise awareness about the problem of world hunger and how one can help. The class should follow through with one of the ideas and help. **Assess** by having students choose an activity and write up how they could tackle it.

Invite organizations through which we can display generosity (Dotson & Dotson, 1997). Invite someone from a non-profit organization such as the United Way, a foundation, or another such organization to speak to the class about what they do and how they are funded. Ask the speaker to talk about the importance of volunteers in such organizations.

Investigate a charitable organization (Dotson & Dotson, 1997). Identify a charitable organization that depends on generosity to stay in business and write a report on this group. What goods or services does it provide? Where does it get funding?

Write a story of a person who refuses to share resources. Write a fictional story about a person who refuses to share. Cause something to happen in the story that changes this person's attitude. **Assess** with report.

Planning service learning. Have students identify needs and develop a plan to provide service to meet the need(s). Have them also include in their service project plan a component which brings them together after having done the service to reflect on what they learned.

Starred activities within each subskill go together!

Being a Community Member by Sharing Resources

Ideas for Developing Skills

Level 3 (continued)

Conduct or participate in a food drive (Dotson & Dotson, 1997). Encourage participation in a canned food drive at your school. Point out to students that they don't need money to serve others.

Respectful service. Students write skits that teach a lesson about helping another person respectfully and act it out. The skit can include issues related to the repercussions of helping in a disrespectful manner.

Level 4: Integrate Knowledge and Procedures

Execute plans, Solve problems

Implementing the plan to share resources. Students, having identified a resource they want to share in a particular situation or with a particular person or group, act on their plan. Students practice sharing their identified resource and report on the experience.

Adopt a child/family (from Dotson & Dotson, 1997). Ask your students if they would like to adopt a child in another country. Figure out what it would cost to do this and make sure that your students are willing to bring in the money. Have the students write a letter to the child. Alternatively, you could ask the students to adopt a needy family for the holiday. Have the class talk about what they want to provide for that family and divide up the responsibilities. (You might wish to make sure that the needy family does not have children at your school.)

Be generous (Dotson & Dotson, 1997). Choose a way to be generous with your time at home. Remember the definition of generous—willing to share. **Assess** by reporting to the class on how you shared your time.

Mount a donation drive. Students put together a coat, shoe, toy or eyeglasses drive in your region. Students ask other students to bring in an item in good condition to donate to the drive. Invite a representative from the responsible organization to speak or write a letter to the school telling them where their donations went. **Assess** with letters.

Starred activities
within each subskill
go together!

Being a Community Member by Sharing Resources

Ideas for Developing Skills

Level 4 (continued)

Implement a service-learning project plan (Dotson & Dotson, 1997). Students, having identified a need and a service project to respond to it, now implement their project. Upon completion of the project include a time for reflection on the activity and what they learned from it.

Conduct a blood drive. Students invite the Red Cross to the school and assist them in collecting blood from volunteer donors. Students can also contribute time to advertising the event and volunteering during the drive itself.

Serving the less fortunate. Select a way to help the less fortunate in the community. For ideas for teens, go to http://www.bygpub.com/books/tg2rw/volunteer.htm.

Assessment Hints

Share Resources

Essays or Oral Reports. Have students write an essay or give an oral report about what they've learned about sharing resources, and give an example of a particularly generous person in their lives.

Interview. Assess an interview by having the students report back to the class, either in a written report or orally, what they talked about and learned from the interview.

List of Exemplars. Assess by having the students, individually or in small groups, create a list of those who have demonstrated impressive generosity, whether in their lives or from the wider culture.

Group Presentations. Have the students break up into small groups and present to the class on what it means to share resources, whether individually or globally, and who might be in particular need of them.

Group Service Project. Have the students come up with and execute a class service project.

Skits. Have the students, in small groups, write a skit and act out the roles of the characters demonstrating what they've discussed and learned about choosing service.

Starred activities within each subskill go together!

Create a Climate
to Develop Responsibility

- Provide many opportunities to engage in prosocial behavior in the classroom.
- Point out the virtues of being helpful.
- Heighten awareness of how each student can help others.
- Model being helpful to others.
- Discuss different ways that people are helpful to others generally.
- Build in opportunities for students to share resources and to offer service.
- Expect students to act thoughtfully towards one another.
- Have a class discussion of ways to act thoughtfully towards one another.

Selections to Post in the Classroom
for Developing Responsibility

Post the word "Mentors" on a bulletin board and have students create posters, pictures, etc. depicting the mentors in their lives.

"Lives of Service" can be displayed on a bulletin board with pictures, or names, of people who have given their lives in service to others, e.g., political figures, religious leaders, local personalities, etc.

Rules for speaking kindly (Forni, 2002)

- Never yell at any one.
- Keep the volume of your voice appropriate for the situation.
- Convey respect with your tone of voice.
- Don't use profanity.
- When you are angry, be civil.
- Never use slurs against a person's identity.

Sample Student Self-Monitoring

Acting Responsibly

Encourage active learning by having students learn to monitor their own learning

Cooperate

I notice what behaviors hurt other people and avoid those behaviors.

I know how to work with others in a group:

Take turns talking.

Take turns being leader.

Take turns being the recorder.

I listen.

Act Thoughtfully

I know how to pick up signals in a conversation about what is comfortable for the other person.

I try not to disturb others.

I watch how much noise I make.

I groom myself in private.

I don't impose myself on others.

Share Resources

I observe others to see how I can help them.

I volunteer to help others without being asked.

I share fairly.

Choose Service

I verify that they would like help.

I know how to be helpful without being patronizing.

Finding Meaning in Life

(Make Meaning)

WHAT

Finding meaning in life can be cultivated through teaching students (1) how to center themselves, (2) how to find and work on commitment to good causes, and (3) how to appreciate aesthetic experiences. Centering is the constant practice of calming inner turmoil, relaxing energy and focusing attention. Commitment means dedicating oneself to something wholeheartedly.

WHY

In order to live a fulfilling life, we need to have something that grounds our being, that is the center of our energies. Commitments shape our goals, our plans, our futures. Humans respond positively to deep beauty—it brings joy and inspiration.

SUBSKILLS OVERVIEW

Center Yourself
Cultivate Commitment
Cultivate Wonder

"Sometimes we confuse having fun with being happy. Being happy is virtually impossible without a history of restraint and discipline. Sometimes in order to reach happiness we must forego fun."
(Forni, 2002, p. 21)

Web Wise

Association for Applied and Therapeutic Humor:
http://www.aath.org
Lesson plans about peace, war, conflict and other topics:
http://www.esrnational.org
www.simpleliving.net

Finding Meaning by Centering Yourself

Creative and Expert Implementer Real-life Example

Ricky Martin, the Latino pop star, spends a great deal of time in meditation and self-reflection. At one point in his career, he took off several months to devote his time entirely to greater self-awareness and spiritual connectedness.

His Holiness the ***Dalai Lama***, exiled leader of Tibet, won the 1989 Nobel Peace Prize because "the Dalai Lama in his struggle for the liberation of Tibet consistently has opposed the use of violence. He has instead advocated peaceful solutions based upon tolerance and mutual respect in order to preserve the historical and cultural heritage of his people." He accepted the prize on behalf of oppressed everywhere and all those who struggle for freedom and work for world peace and the people of Tibet.

Ideas for Developing Skills

Level 1: Immersion in Examples and Opportunities
Attend to the big picture, Learn to recognize basic patterns

Using journals to increase self-awareness. Discuss how people use journals to know themselves. Read examples to the class, e.g., "Walden Pond," Albert Schweitzer's journals, etc. Discuss ways that the authors might have benefited from their journal writing.

What am I like? Have students consider what they are like in different situations. For example, at a party, are they outgoing or shy? At a family gathering, are they active or passive? Have them keep a journal for a week.

Conversation about self-awareness. Select several media personalities who exhibit personal awareness and show the students these examples. Discuss what characteristics the students notice among the personalities who reveal self-awareness. Have students identify other examples from movies, TV, and cartoons who appears to know well his or her capabilities, and who does not.

Experts in self-awareness. Students interview counselors or counseling psychologists. Ask questions like: What is self-awareness? What does one do to become more self aware? What are the benefits of self-awareness?

Role models for centering. Present students with examples of people who focus on being centered. Read excerpts from their work. For example: Dalai Lama, Thomas Merton, Annie Dillard.

Community members who center as part of their lifestyles. Invite guest speakers from religious and spiritual communities or from stressful professions to talk about how they center themselves (e.g., as they start the day, when they get upset, when they need to let go of stress). Ask them to demonstrate or show students how they might use one of their techniques.

Starred activities within each subskill go together!

Learn to play. Some argue that play is vital to human flourishing at any age. Children learn from play. Adult inventors use play as a means of discovery. For information to use in a jigsaw activity, see the Association for Applied and Therapeutic Humor website: http://www.aath.org/

Finding Meaning by Centering Yourself
Ideas for Developing Skills
Level 1 (continued)

Spiritual leaders of the past. (1) Present readings or films on historical examples of leaders who were known for their centering such as Jesus, Mohammed, Buddha. Study their techniques for centering themselves. (2) Bring in experts to discuss the leaders and their approaches.

Ways of letting go. (1) Defining. Research the library, internet, etc. to find information about how people let go and why. (2) Guest speakers: Invite community members who have recovered from trauma or addiction and ask them what letting go means to them, why they do, and how.

Level 2: Attention to Facts and Skills
Focus on detail and prototypical knowledge, Build knowledge

Consider those whom they know who know themselves. Ask the students to pick one person in his or her life who is very self-aware, someone who seems to know him or herself well.

How do we become more self-aware? Have students research different ways people become more aware of themselves. They should provide an example of the method in practice. After the class discusses all the methods, each student can select one to practice for a week. 

Brainstorm about the pitfalls of lacking self-awareness. Brainstorm with the class some possible scenarios that could play out if one were completely lacking in self-awareness. How might it affect their relationships? Their job prospects?

Report on world religions. Break the students into groups and have each of the groups take up one major world religion and investigate how it views self-awareness, and how one might attain it in that particular context, i.e. prayer, meditation, fasting, etc.

Study a role model. Have students select a specific person who is known for centering and being centered and study them in depth. They should write an essay about what the person does to center and what the effects are on the person and on others.

Try yoga. Invite a local expert (or use a video) to show students a few positions in Yoga. Ask students to research the benefits of Yoga and similar exercise.

The power of silence. Have students investigate the use of silence in the world's spiritual and religious traditions. Identify what characteristics are common across all the traditions investigated.

Starred activities within each subskill go together!

Finding Meaning by Centering Yourself

Ideas for Developing Skills

Level 2 (continued)

Relaxation-visualization. Use a relaxation-visualization exercise with the students to help them calm distractions, gather their energy and relax. Relaxation is a skill that can be developed. Some people learn quickly, others take longer. Tell students that they are practicing a skill that will come in handy the rest of their lives (e.g., to stimulate creativity, to increase health by releasing stress). Tell them to keep trying if they are unsuccessful initially. Here is an example of what you might say. Remember to speak slowly and to breathe deeply yourself as you speak.

Find a comfortable position. Close your eyes and take a deep breath. As you breathe, breathe in relaxation and breathe out tension (repeat). As you breathe out tension and breathe in relaxation, you feel lighter and lighter. First, your feet and legs feel relaxed and light...then your abdomen... then your arms and hands....then your neck and head. You feel so light that you begin to float....like a bubble... safely and securely. You float up, up, up.... out of the building and up into the sky. You float freely and safely. You begin to float towards a place that is very relaxing...maybe an island...maybe a mountain...maybe a lake or ocean. You float towards this place and gently land. This place is full of love and energy for you. Breathe it in. (You may have them explore the area and find either a secret treasure that they store in their body and take with them or some course information that you recite or describe.) When you have been filled completely with the love and energy of this place, you begin to float towards the sky again. You float back towards this place....safely and securely...and when you arrive overhead you gently float down and back into this room. Feel your body [in the chair/on the floor]. When you are ready, open your eyes, relaxed and awake.

Pay attention. (1) Give students scenarios to help them develop awareness of their environs. (2) Have students practice paying attention to everything they say and do. They should always be aware of where they are, what behavior is expected, how their actions might affect others, how others might react, etc.

Perspectives on harmony with others. (1) Present readings on being in harmony with others. (2) Have students investigate how spiritual leaders work at being in harmony with others. For example, some people pray for others during prayer and meditation. This includes people they love and people they hate.

Level 3: Practice Procedures

Set goals, Plan steps of problem solving, Practice skills

Discuss awareness of the ways we communicate (Dotson & Dotson, 1997). Help heighten self-awareness by discussing the ways we use verbal and non-verbal communication. Role play situations in which non-verbal conflict causes problems and discuss possible ways to control non-verbal reactions.

Starred activities within each subskill go together!

Finding Meaning by Centering Yourself

Ideas for Developing Skills

Level 3 (continued)

Interview someone whom you consider to be self-aware. Have the students seek out a person to interview about self-awareness. Begin by asking the person to give a definition of self-awareness, and to rate themselves on a scale from 1 – 10 (10 being high in self-awareness). Ask them how it affects their life, at home, on the job, in relationships with others. What has helped them to be more self-aware?

Understanding and identifying self-awareness. Have the students form partners to discuss the following: what they consider most important in the area of self-awareness, the top three qualities of a self-aware person, and a real-life example of each quality. Pairs share with the class.

Discuss the relationship between self-awareness and success. Discuss with the students the importance of being self-aware and the links between it and success. Focus on individuals who seem to know their strengths and weaknesses and the ways in which it helped or impeded their performance. **Assess** by having students list the things that they know themselves to be accomplished at as well as the things where they could do better.

Journal practice. Have each student keep a journal for five minutes to begin or end each day or week. Have students think about particular events and write about their feelings.

Finding inner peace. (1) Have students investigate methods for finding inner peace. Have them report on these and demonstrate. (2) Have students practice the centering techniques of their role model.

Focus on gratitude. (1) Have students interview community members about the things they are grateful for. (2) Have students make a list of everything that they are grateful for.

Centering in a particular domain. Ask professionals to come to class who center themselves for the purpose of getting their work done (e.g., emergency care personnel, police, etc.). Ask them to describe what they do to center and when.

Community centers. Find resources in the community for centering. These might include alternative healing centers or spiritual retreat centers. Visit the centers to find out more about them, to get a demonstration, and to try it out.

Reflect on a passage. Read a simple passage from someone in the field you teach. Ask students to reflect on the meaning and impact of the thoughts. Have students relate the reading to their lives and their studies.

Starred ★ activities within each subskill go together!

Finding Meaning by Centering Yourself

Ideas for Developing Skills

Level 4: Integrate Knowledge and Procedures
Execute plans, Solve problems

An exercise of monitoring personal behavior. Have students use a set of questions to ask themselves at the end of each day which help them to be more self-aware. Areas such as courtesy, diligence, and respect, among others, can be addressed in these questions. **Assess** by incorporating this activity into a journal activity. Collect journals periodically for review.

Practice meditation. Have students find out about their tradition's form of meditation and/or prayer. Ask them to get a coach and set a schedule for practice. Have the coach report on progress.

Practice *ahimsa* as Gandhi did (Altman, 1980). *Ahimsa* means dynamic compassion. It is practicing inner harmony and outer peaceful compassion. A person who practices *ahimsa* does not coerce or manipulate others, does not gratify the ego, does not hurt others in obvious ways (e.g., cruelty nor nonobvious ways (e.g., by being self-centered, greedy, dishonest). *Ahimsa* has four principles: (a) Dynamic compassion (e.g., respecting and furthering life instead of limiting it or destroying it). (b) Nonresistance to evil (i.e., combating injustice with active love or agape to win an opponent over through patience, sympathy or self-suffering). (c) Nonviolent direct personal action (e.g., peaceful demonstrations, risking one's life for others). (d) Noncooperation (respectful disobedience to an unjust law or command).

Choose to live a simpler life (Elgin, 1993). Students select several of the following actions to maintain for a month or more. Have them keep a journal and report on the difficulties and successes. (1) Spend your time outside of work and school in volunteer service, working for justice in the community or in simple activities with friends and family (e.g., walking, making music). (2) Work on developing yourself to full potential (e.g., emotionally, mentally, physically, spiritually). (3) Cultivate a concern for the earth and reverence for nature. (4) Cultivate a concern for the world's poor. (5) Lower your level of consumption (buy fewer clothes, etc.). (6) Purchase things that are durable. (6) Shift your diet away from processed and fast foods to simpler, healthy foods. (7) Reduce clut ter and complexity in your life by giving away things you don't use much. (8) Boycott the products of unethical companies. (9) Recycle as much as you can. (10) Develop personal skills that increase self-reliance for basic needs (e.g., carpentry, plumbing, repair). (11) Support smaller, community-focused businesses and activities. (12) Adopt flexible sex roles. (13) Use transportation that does less harm to the planet.

Assessment Hints

Center Yourself

Essays or Oral Reports. Have students write an essay or give an oral report about what they've learned about self-awareness and who is a particularly good example of it in their lives.

Journaling. Over a period of time, perhaps a week, have students record daily measures of their own self-awareness with regard to such things as courtesy, diligence, timeliness, respect, etc.

Completion of a mentorship. Have students complete a mentorship with a mentor who can guide the student on a regular basis on being focused.

Participation in centering activities. Have students join in relaxation, meditation, or prayer group to center themselves on meaning in their lives.

Finding Meaning by Cultivating Commitment

Creative and Expert Implementer Real-life Example

Joan of Arc began having visions at age 13. Through them she felt called to lead the French people in battle against the English occupation army. She convinced the heir to the French throne to let her lead a battle. At age 16, she did and was victorious. She was captured, imprisoned and brought to trial by her enemies. She was charged with blasphemy, making claims that she had been charged by messengers of God. As she was about to be burned at the stake she forgave her enemies.

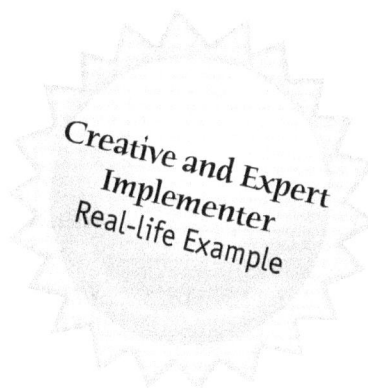

Ideas for Developing Skills

Level 1: Immersion in Examples and Opportunities
Attend to the big picture, Learn to recognize basic patterns

Types of commitments/ ground projects. (1) Examples. Present multiple examples of persons who show deep commitment to positive causes. (2) Interviews. Have students interview community members who are admired for their strong commitments. (3) Speakers. Invite community members to speak about how their commitments influence everything they do.

Making and keeping promises. Read or watch a story about promises kept or broken. Discuss with the students how a promise is a type of commitment and how they shouldn't make promises they don't plan to keep.

What is our purpose in life? Have students investigate different ideas about the purpose of life. Students could investigate: (1) celebrities, (2) officials, (3) historical people, (4) community members, (5) religious leaders. Have students compare perspectives on the purpose of life and how it affects behavior and life choices.

What do people really care about? Have students investigate different ideas about what people really care about. Students could investigate: (1) celebrities, (2) officials, (3) historical people, (4) community members, (5) religious leaders. Have students compare perspectives on what's cared about and how it affects behavior and life choices.

Level 2: Attention to Facts and Skills
Focus on detail and prototypical examples, Build knowledge

Creating good. (1) Have students find examples of people who focus on fostering good around them. What do they do? What don't they do? What are the effects? (2) Have students figure out what action might be needed locally. (3) Have students apply one of the actions or activities they discovered in their investigation.

Starred activities within each subskill go together!

Finding Meaning by Cultivating Commitment

Ideas for Developing Skills

Level 2 (continued)

Non-violence. (1) Have students find examples of people who focus on fostering nonviolence around them. What do they do? What don't they do? What are the effects? (2) Have students figure out what action might be needed locally. (3) Have students apply one of the actions or activities they discovered in their investigation.

Why do people tire of life? Have students gather information about why people might tire of life and analyze what it is they are missing. Have students brainstorm on how to alleviate the issues of people who are discouraged or depressed. Present a report or make a poster about the findings.

Eco-commitment. (1) Have students find examples of people who focus on preserving the environment. What do they do? What don't they do? What are the effects? (2) Have students figure out what action might be needed locally. (3) Have students apply one of the actions or activities they discovered in their investigation.

Avoid hate. Study the life philosophy of a peacemaker like Martin Luther King Jr. The following is an excerpt from Ansbro's (2000) *Martin Luther King, Jr.*, (pp. 231 – 232):

King consistently condemned violence as both immoral and impractical. It is immoral because it thrives on hatred rather than love. It wants to humiliate the opponent rather than to win his understanding. It seeks to injure rather than to redeem the other. Violence is opposed to creativity and wholeness, aims to destroy community, and renders brotherhood impossible. "Like an unchecked cancer, hate corrodes the personality and eats away its vital unity." King identified with Booker T. Washington's warning, "Let no man pull you so low as to make you hate him." King contended that when another makes you hate him, he leads you to work against community and to defy creation. Through his hate the hater becomes depersonalized because the design of creation demands that personality can be fulfilled only in community:

Hate is rooted in fear, and the only cure for fear-hate is love. Hatred and bitterness can never cure the disease of fear; only love can do that. Hatred paralyzes life; love releases it. Hatred confuses life; love harmonizes it. Hatred darkens life; love illuminates it.

Level 3: Practice Procedures

Set goals, Plan steps of problem solving, Practice skills

Commitment in volunteerism. Have students find examples of local persons who are highly committed to volunteering. Have students investigate and report on what the commitment looks like (e.g., long hours of work, persistence at a particular task, not giving up hope). Have students work with one of the people once or longer.

Finding Meaning by Cultivating Commitment

Ideas for Developing Skills

Level 3 (continued)

Work with role model of commitment. Have students select a local community member whose commitment they want to imitate. Have them spend a day or several hours together. Students report on what they did, how the adult demonstrated commitment.

Being a positive influence. (1) Have students find examples of local people who focus on fostering being a positive influence. What do they do? What don't they do? What are the effects? (2) Have students work with a local person as an assistant.

Commitment within a domain. Have students find examples of persons who are highly committed to their work (e.g., in science, social services, education, sport, craftsmanship). Have students investigate and report on what the commitment looks like (e.g., long hours of work, persistence at a particular task, not giving up hope). Students may find local representatives or find them through library/internet research. Have students select one of the behaviors to imitate for a period of time in a particular area.

Commitment to human rights. What does it mean to be committed to human rights? (a) Ask students to identify different perspectives on human rights (e.g., what does China consider human rights? What does the USA consider human rights? What does the Netherlands consider human rights?). How successful are societies that claim to support human rights? They can also consult the United Nations Declaration of Human Rights. (b) Identify local areas of need in terms of human rights. (c) With the help of local community leaders, identify ways that these needs might be alleviated and how students can become involved in bringing about change.

Level 4: Integrate Knowledge and Procedures

Execute plans, Solve problems

Self discipline. Self discipline is required for commitment. Have students identify an area in which they need more discipline. Have them develop a strategic plan for practicing self discipline.

Developing a vision of peace and justice. Have students work with a local exemplar to develop a vision for local peace and justice.

Practicing commitment. Have students identify an area in which they want to practice commitment. Help them identify someone who is an expert in this type of commitment who can be asked to mentor the student for a period of time. Have the student practice the commitment under the coaching of the exemplar.

Cultivate Commitment

Journaling. Over a period of time, perhaps a week, have students record journal entries about what commitments the student has and how they support them.

Reports on experts. Have students write reports on the commitments exemplified by leaders in various fields.

Essays. Have students write an essay on the different ways people show and have commitment in the lives.

Finding Meaning by Cultivating Wonder

Creative and Expert Implementer Real-life Example

Lady Bird Johnson launched the first legislative campaign by a First Lady, the Highway Beautification Act of 1965. As she traveled around the U.S. in the 1960s, she noticed the increasing number of billboards that were spreading along the nation's roads. She saw her advocacy for conservation and beautification of national resources as part of her husband's vision of the Great Society.

Ideas for Developing Skills

Level 1: Immersion in Examples and Opportunities
Attend to the big picture, Learn to recognize basic patterns

Noticing beauty. Take the students to a location that has natural beauty. Have them point out what is beautiful about it. Have each student write about that which they find to be most beautiful element of the location and why. Have them include in their reports a comment on the value in protecting such sites. **Assess** with reports.

Getting in touch with the creative process. Bring in speakers from creative areas of work (e.g., painting, composing, writing, architecture, landscaping, carpentry) and ask them to describe their creative process.

Creating with your hands. In relation to the academic unit you are studying, give students the opportunity to make (a) a food like bread or jam or another basic food, or (b) some kind of useful product.

Creating with your mind. In relation to the academic unit you are studying, give students the opportunity to create visual art, poetry, music, stories, or an invention.

Human-made world. Bring in examples of well-designed things that are related to the subject you teach. Ask students what makes a good design? Discuss the principles of good design for the things you brought in (do a search on the web).

The natural world and the unnatural world. Discuss what is natural and what is unnatural in terms of basic human needs (e.g., nourishment, sleep, shelter, clothing, love and friendship) and in terms of products and transportation.

Starred activities within each subskill go together!

Learn to play. Some argue that play is vital to human flourishing at any age. Children learn from play. Adult inventors use play as a means of discovery. For information to use in a jigsaw activity, see the Association for Applied and Therapeutic Humor website: http://www.aath.org/

Finding Meaning by Cultivating Wonder
Ideas for Developing Skills
Level 1 (continued)

Noticing beauty. Help students notice the beauty of natural things of well-designed human artifacts.

What are aesthetics? Bring in speakers to talk about aesthetics in their lines of work. What are the ideals in their line of work? How do they promote aesthetics?

How do people experience wonder? Read excerpts from writers about their wonder (e.g., Annie Dillard). Domains include science, writing, fine arts, sport, business, education, craftsmanship.

Experiencing wonder. Set up ways for students to experience wonder in the domain you teach.

Wonder in a particular domain. Bring in guest speakers from different lines of work and ask them to describe what kinds of wonder and joy they experience in their work.

Level 2: Attention to Facts and Skills
Focus on detail and prototypical examples, Build knowledge

How do people attempt to create beauty? Students interview people who seek to create beauty (e.g., designers, artists, musicians, dancers) and ask them to identify the important features of their work. Have the students consider, if they could be any sort of artist/designer, what would they choose to be? What medium would they take up?

Sense for a day. After presenting examples of your own or from others, ask students to pay attention to what their senses experience of the natural world throughout a day (senses include: Taste, Touch, Smell, Sight, Sound, Movement). Ask them to journal on the experience and share excerpts with the class.

Connecting to the world with our senses. Study the ways that communities and cultures within the country enjoy their senses. Study other cultures' views of what is sensually good

My favorite sensing. Bring in an example of a favorite way to connect to the natural world through one of your senses and ask students to do the same. Discuss sensing in relation to the subject you teach.

Starred activities within each subskill go together!

What is beautiful? Discuss how people decide what is beautiful. Ask students to interview community members on what they think is beautiful (you might want to specify the domain, such as what is a beautiful neighborhood) and what they do to make beauty in the world. Report and discuss.

Finding Meaning by Cultivating Wonder

Ideas for Developing Skills

Level 2 (continued)

Music, the senses and the natural world. (1) Listening. Listen in class to some natural 'song' such as whale song or wolf howling. Ask students to listen quietly, draw or write during the songs. (2) In class jam assignment. Ask students to bring in a natural sound—sample it on tape or bring it in to make the sound live. Decide how to 'run' the orchestra and have a jam session. You may supplement with recorded music. (3) Ask students to keep track of the 'natural music' they hear everyday like birdsong, wind, rain, etc.

Visions, the senses and the natural world. (1) Visual art. Bring in examples of beautiful visual art. Ask students to reflect quietly as they study the art. Ask them to react in some way such as writing. Then discuss what they liked. (2) Poetry. Read poems about the environment by W.H. Auden, Gary Snyder, or Denise Levertov (or other poet). Ask students to write their own poems. (3) Photography. Bring in photos (or look at them on the web) that strike the senses (e.g., shocking photos could be of the hundred slain buffalo, lynchings or Dorothea Lang's photos of poverty; beautiful photos could be of trees or landscapes). Ask students to take them seriously and feel their feelings. Ask them to write about the experience.

Where do we go when we die? One of the things humans wonder about is death and afterlife. Bring in guest speakers to discuss these questions from local churches and relevant organizations (e.g., hospice, medicine). Ask students to write an essay about what they believe.

Level 3: Practice Procedures

Set goals, Plan steps of problem solving, Practice skills

Creating beauty. Students create a plan to create beauty in the classroom and school. Either individually, or in small groups, they should come up with at least three concrete things which would enhance their classroom environment, and three things which would contribute to the beauty of the entire school.

Fostering wonder in others. (1) Invite artists, musicians, magicians, and mystics. Invite local community members to speak about how they cultivate a sense of wonder. (2) Ask the guests to coach the students on fostering wonder in themselves or others.

Practicing wonder. Have students choose an activity to practice their sense of wonder: (a) contemplating nature, (b) listening to beautiful uplifting music, (c) camping, (d) going into the wilderness, (e) stargazing away from light pollution, (f) hiking outside of the city or town, (g) watching a movie of beauty like Baraka, (h) growing things.

Finding Meaning by Cultivating Wonder

Ideas for Developing Skills

Level 4: Integrate Knowledge and Procedures

Execute plans, Solve problems

I create beauty. Each student identifies ways that he or she can create beauty and sets goals to do so. This can include the classroom environment and/or the school as a whole. You might consider having different groups take different areas. Students should implement their plans. **Assess** with a report on implemented plan.

Creating wonder for others. Have students work with an expert to create and present a show of 'wonder' for young children.

Creating beauty in the community. Have students interview local community members of all ages and stations to assess what areas of the community are ugly and need beautifying and what might be done. Have students work with community businesses on beautifying one or more locations.

Assessment Hints

Cultivate Wonder

Observation journal. Have students spend five minutes in silence in different environments during which they observe their surroundings. Afterwards they write down their experience.

Participation in beautification activities. Have students participate in beautification activities such as picking up litter, creating a mural.

Reports. Have students report on wonders in the local community.

Creative work. Have students write poems, plays, musical compositions, art that represent the student's sense of wonder.

Create a Climate
to Find Meaning in Life

- Verbalize the benefit of prosocial action for others.
- Promote an atmosphere of fairness and equality.
- Establish the classroom as a considerate and sensitive community.
- Model gratitude.
- Encourage gratitude as a helpful and healthy attitude.
- Discuss and promote peaceful ways of solving problems.
- Avoid and discourage cynical attitudes towards the good things in life.
- Create a beautiful environment in the classroom as much as possible (ask the art teacher for help if you need it).
- Discuss the things that put you in awe, the things that move you, the things that fill you with wonder, the things that you find deeply beautiful.

Sample Student Self-Monitoring
Finding Meaning in Life

Encourage active learning by having students learn to monitor their own learning

Center Yourself
I think about my ideal self when I make decisions.
I think about my values and principles when I make decisions.
I reflect on how I have behaved according to my values.
I know ways to center myself.
I can center myself.
I can take deep breaths when I get upset.
Cultivate Commitment
I have positive commitments.
I have goals for my life.
I can use self-discipline to reach my goals.
Cultivate Wonder
I nurture the sense of wonder in others.
I nurture the sense of wonder in myself.
I try to make a place more beautiful than it was when I found it.

Valuing Traditions and Institutions

(Value social structures)

WHAT

Valuing traditions and institutions means respecting the laws, practices, and organizations of one's society. Respecting them requires an awareness of traditions and the functions of institutions. Members of democratic societies in democracies are obligated to be active citizens and to know the skills that are required for full participation.

WHY

Having a positive feeling toward the laws, practices and organizations of society can lead to increased participation in community decision making. A democracy is only as good as the citizens that create it. Active citizenship can lead to a motivation to help others and an ability to find the resources needed to get the job done.

A student who feels part of a system that is supportive may be more likely to feel that he or she can help another person. In other words, if the student feels supported by society and has a general level of trust in societal forces then he can "afford" to extend him or herself to benefit another person. Conversely, if the student has developed a negative attitude toward the society, and feels unsupported, then he or she may feel the need to satisfy his or her own needs first, possibly at the cost of others.

SUBSKILLS

Identify and Value Traditions
Understand Social Structures
Practice Democracy

Web Wise

Lesson plans about peace, war, conflict and other topics at www.esrnational.org

A website that connects classrooms around the world, students to world expeditions: www.gsn.org

Resources and information about Native Americans: www.nativeweb.org

Valuing Traditions by Identifying Them

Creative and Expert Implementer Real-life Example

Senator ***Robert Byrd*** of Virginia is widely known as the "Dean of the Senate." He is well read in its history and is respected for attempting to honor its history by maintaining decorum and respect for the institution.

Ideas for Developing Skills

Level 1: Immersion in Examples and Opportunities

Attend to the big picture, Learn to recognize basic patterns

Community traditions. Have students interview local community leaders to find out about the traditional ways of organizing the neighborhood(s), fostering change, supporting neighbors, helping the less fortunate, etc.

Holiday traditions. Have the students find out about local holiday traditions. For example, what do people do to celebrate the 4th of July? What are some of the varying family customs around the celebration of Christmas, Hanukah, or Ramadan? Why might traditions differ among families? Why do they become important?

The successful marriage (Dotson & Dotson, 1997). Interview a couple who have been married for more than ten years. Ask them what characteristics they think are important in helping them stay together. **Assess** with a report on your interview.

Respect for my culture. Students interview elders in their communities about the community's customs and traditions. How do they honor the traditions and customs? How do people of different age groups honor them? What are the benefits of these traditions and customs? Students report on their findings.

Level 2: Attention to Facts and Skills

Focus on detail and prototypical knowledge, Build knowledge

Local customs (Dotson & Dotson, 1997). Have the students find out about local customs (e.g. holiday parades, annual school events, local cultural festivals, etc.). Why are they important for the community? For whom might they have particular importance?

Valuing family. Research your family name by interviewing family members or using other resources. See if you can find out its origin and meaning. **Assess** with a report summarizing what you found.

Starred activities within each subskill go together!

Valuing Traditions by Identifying Them

Ideas for Developing Skills

Level 2 (continued)

Investigate traditions. Have the students investigate the roots of various traditions (e.g., wedding rituals, holiday customs, family traditions, etc.). Encourage a conversation about the importance of these traditions. **Assess** by having the students report on what they've learned.

Level 3: Practice Procedures

Set goals, Plan steps of problem solving, Practice skills

Involvement in community traditions. After interviewing local community leaders to find out about the traditional ways of organizing the neighborhood(s), fostering change, supporting neighbors, and helping the less fortunate, have the students investigate how they can get involved in such organizations.

Practicing a tradition. Students select a tradition in which they would like to get involved (e.g., attending the meeting of a social club or order, participating in an Irish dance class, cooking an ethnic specialty, etc.). Have them report back to class on their experience.

Trying different traditions. Students identify a tradition outside their own and participate. Have them interview those who continue the tradition. Have them report back to the class on their experience and on the importance of the particular tradition to those who continue to honor it.

Level 4: Integrate Knowledge and Procedures

Execute plans, Solve problems

Leading a tradition. Have the students take charge of an old tradition in the school or neighborhood. Have them investigate its importance before taking it on, and then put them in charge of conducting it for a period of time. Encourage them to reflect on why people might value this particular tradition.

Adapting a tradition. Encourage the students to investigate traditions of other cultures and societies and adapt it for a classroom or school activity. Have a group or the whole class be the planning team and include in the event as many educational elements as possible. Invite those who are of that culture, or who have been helpful in educating the students about the particular tradition, to the event.

Starred activities within each subskill go together!

Identify and Value Traditions

Essays or Oral Reports. Have students write an essay or give an oral report about what they've learned about the importance of identifying and valuing institutions.

Group Project/Activity. Assess a project activity in which students take action to promote a valuing of institutions by visiting a local institution, by observing their level of participation.

Interview. Assess an interview by having the students report back to the class, either in a written report or orally, what they talked about and learned from the interview.

Valuing Institutions by Understanding Social Structures

Creative and Expert Implementer Real-life Example

Kofi Anan, a graduate of Macalester College in St. Paul, Minnesota, is General Secretary of the most widely known international organization in the world, the United Nations. Effectiveness in his position requires that he have a keen understanding of social structures and traditions of peoples, cultures, and nations all over the world.

Ideas for Developing Skills

Level 1: Immersion in Examples and Opportunities
Attend to the big picture, Learn to recognize basic patterns

Taking a look at non-profit organizations. Students interview or correspond with leaders in non-profit groups to find out how they accomplish their goals. How do they view their work in terms of constitutionality? How do they benefit society?

International structures. Divide the class into groups and have each group research the role and structures of international groups such as UNESCO, the United Nations, UNICEF, etc. What is the mission of each group? How does each benefit society?

Social structures in action. Visit a social institution such as a hospital, a police station, a traffic control center, or a city council meeting. Students keep notes on what benefits the institution brings to the citizens and later discuss the experience. Assess with an essay after the discussion.

Level 2: Attention to Facts and Skills
Focus on detail and prototypical knowledge, Build knowledge

Classroom discussion about social structures. Facilitate a classroom discussion to answer the following questions: What are social structures? Which of them do you participate in, either actively or passively? How do they benefit society?

Consider a world. Encourage the class to consider a world where we did not value and sustain social structures. What would it mean for society? Who would lead? Who would follow? Lead the discussion toward a greater appreciation of social structures and their contribution to the common good and social order.

Starred activities within each subskill go together!

Valuing Institutions by Understanding Social Structures

Ideas for Developing Skills

Level 2 (continued)

Understanding the responsibilities of citizenship (Dotson & Dotson, 1997). Have students write an essay on what responsibilities they have as citizens of the U.S. This is a free country, but can you do anything you want? Why not? **Assess** by essay.

Team work as a component of effective social structures. Have students work as a team on a project and then lead a discussion on the following questions. How does one's experience on a sports team teach one about effective teamwork in a club or organization? What elements of a successful athletic team might inform and enhance the effectiveness of a social club or group?

Investigate community organizations. Ask each student to investigate a particular community organization, whether local, regional, national or international. Encourage each student to speak to a member of the group, or if not possible, to research the group on the internet or elsewhere. **Assess** by report to the class.

Level 3: Practice Procedures

Set goals, Plan steps of problem solving, Practice skills

Participating in community organizations. Students select a group and become a student or honorary member. The group could be international, national, regional, local non-profit or government related. Students identify how these groups work on the inside. Assess with report to the class.

Visit the local City Hall or government building. Conduct a class activity that visits the local city hall. Have the students arrange a meeting with a city official at that time (i.e., the mayor, city administrator, local ward supervisor, etc.). Ask the official to speak about the importance of social structures/organizations for the common good.

Level 4: Integrate Knowledge and Procedures

Execute plans, Solve problems

Create a mock social organization. Have the students create their own activist social organization to address a particular local need (e.g., conservation, homelessness, public safety, etc). Encourage them to mobilize forces to address the concern, and then to act on the results of the meetings. **Assess** by reporting back on results of efforts. (Note: As a long-term project, this could facilitate opportunities for many other activities or cross-disciplinary learning.)

Starred activities within each subskill go together!

Valuing Institutions by Understanding Social Structures

Ideas for Developing Skills

Level 4 (continued)

Activist participation in a community organization. Students identify an issue (as a whole group, small groups or individuals) in which they want to get involved. Students then join the group as honorary or student members and work on their issue. Report to class on the experience.

Assessment Hints

Understand Social Structures

Essays or Oral Reports. Have students write an essay or give an oral report about what they've learned about the importance of understanding social structures.

Interview. Assess an interview by having the students report back to the class, either in a written report or orally, what they talked about and learned from the interview.

Individual Performance. Following a cooperative or class activity targeting an issue related to understanding social structures, assess students on their individual contribution and performance.

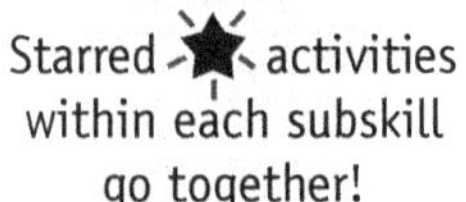
Starred activities
within each subskill
go together!

Valuing Institutions by Practicing Democracy

Creative and Expert Implementer Real-life Example

Susan B. Anthony believed that women should have full citizenship status. She held rallies and gave speeches about the nature of democracy. She and her colleagues were instrumental in persuading the U.S. congress to allow women to express their opinions and vote.

Ideas for Developing Skills

Level 1: Immersion in Examples and Opportunities
Attend to the big picture, Learn to recognize basic patterns

Government in action. Visit a social institution such as a hospital, a police station, a traffic control center, or a city council meeting. Students keep notes on what benefits the institution bring to the citizens and later discuss the experience.

Duties of citizenship. Students interview a government official about the duties of citizenship. Students should consider the ways in which they already fulfill those duties. What privileges must they wait for in order to fulfill other duties (e.g. voting, military service, public office, etc.)?

A story of citizenship (Dotson & Dotson, 1997). Read the story, "The Stone in the Road," which can be found in *The Moral Compass*, by William Bennett. Discuss how actions, not complaints, often get the job done.

Supporting the military (Dotson & Dotson, 1997). Invite an armed services recruiter to speak to the class about the work of the military, and of career options available. **Assess** by having the students write a report on what they heard.

Interview someone who served in the military. Have students interview someone who served in the military. How did they enjoy their experience? Would they encourage it of others.

Understanding taxes (Dotson & Dotson, 1997). Invite an accountant or regional tax official to discuss taxes. Why is it a duty of citizens to pay their taxes? Discuss the goods and services that taxes provide. (Students may be unaware of many of the ways taxes benefit everyone.)

Starred activities within each subskill go together!

Valuing Institutions by Practicing Democracy

Ideas for Developing Skills

Level 2: Attention to Facts and Skills

Focus on detail and prototypical examples, Build knowledge

Essay on government. Have a class discussion on each visit to a social institution. Have each student or group of students write about government and the particular institutional function which they visited or were assigned.

Classroom discussion about government structures. Facilitate a classroom discussion to answer the following questions: What are government structures? Which of them do you participate in, either actively or passively? How do they benefit society?

Discuss freedom of speech (Dotson & Dotson, 1997). Invite a member of the American Civil Liberties Union or a constitutional scholar to discuss the importance of the freedom of speech. Why is this a very important part of our country's identity? How has it been denied people in various places throughout the world throughout history?

Conduct an interview about taxes (Dotson & Dotson, 1997). Ask your parent or guardian how he or she feels about taxes. Do they think taxes are necessary? What percentage of their income goes to taxes? **Assess** with an essay about how the government could get money if it didn't have taxes.

Investigate the life of an American Hero. Invite a local hero or read about one. Why is this person an "American" hero? How does he or she reflect the values of our nation? Would this hero be a hero in any other land or nation?

Study the structure of our local and national government. Have the students do a chart explaining the role of the president, senators, and representatives on the national level, and another of local officials (e.g., mayor, city council members, etc.). Include on the chart the names of the present office-holders in each case. Discuss the roles of each.

Level 3: Practice Procedures

Set goals, Plan steps of problem-solving, Practice skills

Classroom government. Discuss with your students the governing of the classroom. What is required for the good order of the classroom? Who is responsible to see that good order is maintained? Discuss ways to govern the classroom. Implement one or two.

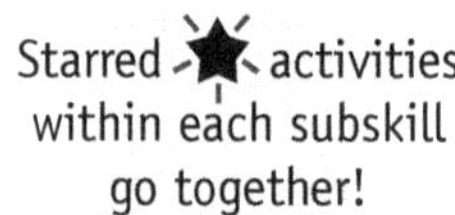
Starred activities within each subskill go together!

Valuing Institutions by Practicing Democracy

Ideas for Developing Skills

Level 3 (continued)

List of duties for a good citizen (Dotson & Dotson, 1997). Design a worksheet on which students list duties of a good citizen. What are we entitled to as citizens of the United States? What are we responsible for? Have students assess themselves on how well they are completing their responsibilities.

Practicing democracy in everyday decisions. First discuss how we exercise democracy when making group decisions, such as choosing a movie to attend. Have students keep a journal on their different experiences of democracy during the week. When they report to the class, have them indicate where democracy could be practiced more or better.

Different governments: An ethical perspective. Have students research different forms of democratic government that exist or have existed around the world and report to class. Does the government act in the best interest of its citizens? If yes, how? If no, why not? Does the government have safeguards to prevent a "bad" idea from becoming law? If yes, what are they? How many people are involved in making decisions for the nation?

Level 4: Integrate Knowledge and Procedures

Execute plans, Solve problems

Community participation. Consider ways in your class that others have contributed to the good order of the community in which they live. Plan how they themselves can contribute to the civic good in solving a local problem. Execute the plan.

Run a mock meeting of the U.S. Senate or House. Have the students run a mock meeting of one of the Houses of Congress. Designate a Speaker, and particular members and reenact a typical gathering in a Congressional chamber debating a bill which addresses a particular issue of concern to the class or the community.

Write letters to political leaders on important local and/or national issue(s). Have the students write letters to their municipal, state or national political leaders about an issue of concern. Read the letter to the class before sending it. Report on reply if and when one is received.

Starred activities within each subskill go together!

Practice Democracy

Essays or Oral Reports. Have students write an essay or give an oral report about what they've learned about the importance of practicing democracy and who is a good exemplar of it.

Checklist of Citizenship. Give the students the opportunity to come up with a list of the qualities and characteristics that describe a good citizen.

Interview. Assess an interview by having the students report back to the class, either in a written report or orally, what they talked about and learned from the interview.

Write a Letter. Have the students write a letter to an elected official expressing concern about an issue of importance to them.

Create a Climate
to Value Traditions and Institutions

(from *Educating for Character*, 1992, p. 100)

Build positive cohesion

- Develop class traditions and symbols.
- Develop each student's feeling of being a unique and valued member of the class community.
- Create accountability to group rules.
- Foster an ethic of interdependence.

Promote knowledge of the system

- Make it explicit what to do when there is an academic problem.
- Make it explicit what to do when there is a social problem.
- Make it explicit what to do when there is a psychological problem.

Understanding of systems

- Provide opportunities for the building of trust among members of the class.
- Encourage trust of rules and systems.
- Make justice/fairness an explicit concern of yours.
- Keep bureaucratic regulations to a minimum.
- Provide resource guides to enable independent resource acquisition.
- Alter infrastructures when they no longer benefit students.
- Maintain a positive community spirit (responsive classroom).
- Establish clear behavior codes (discuss meaning and development of codes).
- Foster peer connections.
- Point to cooperation as an important/amiable characteristic for group projects.

Understanding of Society as a Good

<u>Social Systems.</u> Look at the development of various social systems and how its people translated their values and their needs into social institutions.

Sample Student Self-Monitoring
Valuing Traditions and Institutions

Encourage active learning by having students learn to monitor their own learning

Identify and value traditions
I know my family traditions.
I can identify my religious/spiritual traditions.
I know my community's traditions.
I know my country's traditions.
I respect these traditions.

Understand social structures
I understand how the local government works.
I understand how the state government works.
I understand how the national government works.
I know how to start a petition.
I know how to lodge a complaint against a government agency.
I know how to write a letter to the editor.
I know how the school hierarchy works.
I know how to get to college.
I know how to prepare myself for my future career.
I know how to find help when I need it.

Practicing Democracy
I know how to vote.
I know how to have a political discussion.
I know how to show respect for those who disagree with me.
I know how to write a letter to my representatives.
I know the fair ways to make changes in the laws.
I know how to follow a government meeting.

Selections to Post in the Classroom
for Valuing Traditions and Institutions

(Dotson & Dotson, 1997)

Cut out newspaper articles (or ask students to find them) about good persons in your community who are being good citizens. Use the header, "Meet the good citizens of your town."

Show persons of all colors and nationalities spread across a diagram of the U.S. (Don't forget Hawaii and Alaska.) Use the header, "Liberty and Justice for All."

Ethical Motivation 7

Developing Ethical Identity and Integrity

(Build Integrity)

WHAT

Ethical identity is the perception one has of oneself as an ethical agent. It involves respecting oneself, as well as a positive identification with an ethical role model in order to create a positive ethical identity. Ethical identity motivates ethical action because the person attempts to match an ethical self-concept or ideal with action. The goal of development is to reach one's potential as an ethical, fully functioning individual in community.

WHY

Integrity is rooted in a positive ethical identity. A positive identity leads to more positive behavior. A belief that one is an ethical person leads to more ethical behavior. Ethical identity is heavily influenced by role models. To benefit from an ethical role model, you need to identify with the role model and take on the model's characteristics.

SUBSKILLS OVERVIEW

Choose Good Values
Build Your Identity
Reach for Your Potential

Web Wise

http://www.goodhumans.com/Guidelines/

Find multiple lesson plans with assessments for building character at www.goodcharacter.com

Developing Integrity by Choosing Good Values

Creative and Expert Implementer Real-life Example

Oskar Schindler was a hard-living man, a gambler, a drinker and an adulterer. He was a keen-eyed business man. He followed the Nazis into Poland as a blackmarketeer. He acquired a factory that was run by Jews, whom he treated fairly and kept safe from the Nazis. In 1942, he saw the Nazi raid on a Jewish ghetto where innocent people were packed into trains headed for the death camps. This awoke his sense of justice and resolved to fight the system. He established a 'camp' in his factory and saved over 900 Jews whose names he put on his famous list of workers that he needed for the factory.

Ideas for Developing Skills

Level 1: Immersion in Examples and Opportunities

Attend to the big picture, Learn to recognize basic patterns

What does making good choices mean? A good motive is one where the actor seeks to cause the most good. The wish to do one's duty is the best motive/highest moral value but other motives have high moral value too.

Role models for choosing the good. Show examples of people who focus on choosing the good, either within a difficult situation or in general. These can be (a) local community members, (b) celebrities of present or past (e.g., Audrey Hepburn, Eleanor Roosevelt), (c) fictional characters (e.g., Meg in *A Wrinkle in Time*), (d) Biblical characters. Note the difficulties they faced.

Choosing the good within a particular domain. Present examples of people in a particular domain who chose the good even though not doing so would have been easier or more expedient. Domains can include fields of study and professions such as science, writing, fine arts, sport, business, education, craftsmanship, policing, government.

Choosing what is good for me to flourish. Have students make a list of the kinds of decisions they make everyday. Then discuss what would be good choices and bad choices in terms of helping yourself thrive.

Level 2: Attention to Facts and Skills

Focus on detail and prototypical knowledge, Build knowledge

Making bad choices. Discuss the three types of vicious action (Ross, 1930): desire to do what is wrong, desire to bring about evil, desire to inflict pain on another. Point out, like Ross, that most bad actions are not these but result from self-centeredness. Bad action is bad not usually because it stems from malevolence but because, in search of pleasure, the actor is insensitive to the pain he is causing. Hollywood movies often show characters who are malicious.

Developing Integrity by Choosing Good Values

Ideas for Developing Skills

Level 2 (continued)

Selecting a role model for choosing the good. Have students select an appropriate role model and investigate the life (or particular situation) and experience of the individual. Students report on what obstacles were faced, how the person overcame the obstacles, what the person achieved.

Comparing exemplars. Take a set of exemplars and have students study the similarities and differences among them.

Choosing what is good for human rights. (1) Investigate human rights generally. What does it mean? What do people disagree about it? What does it require of governments, communities and individuals? (2) Investigate human rights in a particular country. (3) Investigate human rights in your local community.

Choosing what is good for civic discourse. Investigate what kinds of individual, group, political, and business decisions contribute to civic discourse? Which ones do not? Interview specialists and regular citizens.

How do we avoid specific evils (e.g., laziness of thinking or doing, failing to help others, carelessness with the environment)? Study the ways that religious community members avoid a specific evil. Help students notice manifestations of this evil in everyday life and media.

Level 3: Practice Procedures

Set goals, Plan steps of problem solving, Practice skills

Cultivating good in a particular domain. Study in detail the goodness that can be cultivated in a particular domain (e.g., science, writing, fine arts, sport, business, education, craftsmanship). This can be done by (a) interviewing experts in the area or (b) studying historical documents. Have students present their findings.

Choosing the good for the environment/global relevance. (1) Investigate what is good for the environment in general. Read a book like *50 ways you can help save the planet* (Campolo & Aeschliman, 1992) or find resources on the web such as long-standing, respected environmental groups (e.g., Audubon Society, Sierra Club, Nature Conservancy, National Resources Defense Council). (2) Find out what environmental issues exist locally. (3) Select an action that you can take to improve the environment locally.

Understanding evil. Present readings on evil (generally or in a particular domain). Have students investigate different views of evil in religious and spiritual traditions. Invite the elders of the community to speak of their experiences of evil.

Developing Integrity by Choosing Good Values

Ideas for Developing Skills

Level 3 (continued)

What is vice? Have students investigate the notion of vice. What actions are included? What is the source of vice? Invite local religious and spiritual leaders to discuss different viewpoints. For examples, some argue (e.g., the philosopher, John Kekes) that one either develops virtue or one develops vice. If one does not focus on the skills outlined in this book, then one is developing vice (habits that cause harm to others).

Truth is good. Present some readings on truth (general readings, or readings in a particular domain such as truth in science). Have students find present-day (or historic) examples of truth and its impact. Discuss how students can contribute to cultivating truth.

Love is good. Present some readings on love. Have students find present-day (or historic) examples of love and its impact. Discuss how students can contribute to cultivating love.

Joy is good. Present some readings on joy. Have students find present-day (or historic) examples of joy and its impact. Discuss how students can contribute to cultivating joy.

What is the good life? Present various viewpoints on the good life. Ask students to analyze what the media says about the good life, and what other messages they get about the good life other places (e.g., at home). Ask the students to compare and contrast these views.

What do people really want? Have students interview elders about what they really value and desire and what they do to get it. Have students compare the elders' responses with their own.

Practice makes perfect. Read a story about a character who practices to achieve a larger, more difficult goal. Explain how practicing by making small ethical choices every day will make it easier for people to choose the ethical option in larger, more difficult issues. Discuss the importance of good habits. Challenge students to set a goal of a new good habit and meet that goal for at least 21 days. (Note: studies indicate that a practice maintained for 21 or more days is likely to become habit.)

Developing Integrity by Choosing Good Values

Ideas for Developing Skills

Level 4: Integrate Knowledge and Procedures

Execute plans, Solve problems

Adult mentor. With the help of an adult mentor, ask students to work at choosing what is good in a particular domain. Ask the mentor to focus on what are the ethical duties in the domain.

Avoiding evil. (1) Discuss what evil is. According to Kekes (1990), evil is undeserved harm. Regular actions of people with defective characters—dominated by vices—are primarily evil and therefore make them evil people. Character morality prescribes a set of practices whose aim is to avoid evil (institutional, moral tradition) and prescribes an attitude to evil—the reflective temper—upon which increasing control over personal conduct depends. Vices do not result from the corruption of virtues, rather from their own cultivation in place of virtue. The source of most evil in the world is in three categories: malevolence (blaming), insufficiency (not reflecting critically) and expediency (harming others when they get in your way). (2) Discuss how people can avoid evil (e.g., by cultivating ethical skills instead of vices). (3) Ask students to assess what evil they are tempted by and ask them to think of alternative actions to replace what is or leads to evil. (4) Ask students to journal on their progress in doing this. If possible enlist a mentor to help them.

Assessment Hints

Choose Good Values

Essays on a personal choice. Have students write an essay about a personal decision and the good and bad options that were considered and why their choice was the best choice.

Essays on another's choice. Have students write an essay about a person or story character's decision-making and rationale for his/her choice.

Advocacy projects. Have students create and participate in advocacy projects in the local community such as creating and presenting public service announcements, speeches on human rights.

Social action projects. Have students create and participate in social action projects to encourage local officials to make good choices, such as petitions, demonstrations, letter writing, advocacy, campaigning.

Developing Integrity by Building Your Identity

Creative and Expert Implementer Real-life Example

Minnesota Vikings' wide receiver ***Chris Carter*** and feminist activist ***Gloria Steinem*** are two people who have made great efforts in creating identities for themselves, and in so doing influenced many people.

Level 1: Immersion in Examples and Opportunities
Attend to the big picture, Learn to recognize basic patterns

Examining stories of positive identity. Read stories that provide examples of ethical motivation that are tied to a person's identity. Discuss the value of acting consistently with one's ethical judgement. When is it hard to do the right thing? What are some of the road blocks the characters faced in trying to complete an ethical action? What are some of the ways the characters in the stories got around or dealt with these difficulties? What are some ways you deal with such difficulties? Students also discuss what actions in the story exemplified skills that are most helpful when trying to complete ethical action (e.g., courage, a sense of commitment to others, etc.). Sample stories can be found at the Character Building website: http://www.uensd.org/USOE_Pages/ic/chared/biographical.html. "George Washington Carver" (a story about curiosity, integrity, love of knowledge, work ethic), "Confucius" (a story about humility and integrity), "Eleanor Roosevelt" (a story about courage, dignity, equality, hard work and self-worth), "Corrie Ten Boom" (a story about ethical courage, integrity, kindness, endurance, empathy).

Stories of honor. Discuss the meaning and manifestation of honor after reading stories like the *Red Badge of Courage* (Crane, 1982). Do they know someone who shows honor in the way that he or she lives life? **Assess** with a report by each student on a person of honor in their lives.

Value identification. Students should find out what the values of family/religion/culture/community are by means of (1) interviews of family or community members, (2) library research, (3) community exploration. They should ask the following questions: What are the standards for behavior? What are obligations vs. personal preferences? With whom does the student identify most?

Discussion of individual uniqueness. Discuss individual uniqueness of each human being. (1) Watch videos of babies and children. Have students discuss how people can vary visibly (e.g., height, weight, hair color) and invisibly (intelligence, motivations, interests). Discuss how people show their uniqueness. (2) Have students write about each others' unique positive qualities on a sheet with everyone's name. Compile these comments and hand them to each student.

Starred activities within each subskill go together!

Developing Integrity by Building Your Identity

Ideas for Developing Skills

Level 1 (continued)

Focusing on respect. Bring in several experts who work with self-respect in their clients, such as counselors, ministers, women's advocates. Ask them to discuss what self-respect means and how they foster it in their clients. Also discuss the relation between self-respect and respect for others.

Draw a scene from your life (Dotson & Dotson, 1997). Draw a scene from your life with the heading, "I respect myself when I..." In this scene, show a time when you did something that gave you self-respect. Assess by creativity and quality of project.

Level 2: Attention to Facts and Skills

Focus on detail and prototypical knowledge, Build knowledge

Stories of positive identity. Take a language arts lesson and remodel it to focus on character. Check comprehension by requiring students to use independent thinking (What is a positive identity? How does the main character reveal his/her positive identity? How do you reveal your positive identity?), analysis of actions (Why does the main character act the ways he does? How do his/her actions relate to his/her positive identity?), and other higher level thinking skills. (See Paul, 1987, *Critical Thinking Handbook*, pp. 136-138, for more ideas).

Looking for positive ethical identities. Students identify features of adults' attitudes and behaviors that reflect a positive ethical identity. Brainstorm about features and about those in their world who embody them.

Valuing the good. Discuss what goodness is, what excellence is. How do people strive for these? Where do you strive for goodness? For excellence (e.g., on sports field)? Is this something that I would be proud of? Is this something my positive hero would be proud of?

Historical values. Understanding that everything you do is driven by one value or another. Needs are interests which are values. What you focus on becomes what you value. Read about historical figures—good and evil people—and what drove them to what they did.

★ **Elements of honor.** Have the students review their own descriptions of honor in their reports on people who seem to portray honor. Identify the characteristics that seem to be inherent in people of honor. What are they? Do I have them?

Starred ★ activities within each subskill go together!

Keeping a healthy choices record. Have students keep a record of their food choices and amount of sleep for one 24-hour period. Discuss what choices show self-respect and which do not.

Developing Integrity by Building Your Identity

Ideas for Developing Skills

Level 2 (continued)

Self-respect and our family (Dotson & Dotson, 1997). Discuss how our families affect our self-respect. Ask students to think of someone in their family histories who had a quality they admire and have them share with the class.

The relationship between prejudices and self-respect (Dotson & Dotson, 1997). Discuss prejudices and self-respect. Are these two attitudes related? Ask students to share examples of prejudices, then look at how these incidents affect self-respect—in both the person feeling the prejudice and the person receiving the prejudice.

Describe a person of self-respect. Present a list of characteristics that describe a person with self-respect, or develop this list with the students. Have students select the characteristics that apply to them and add other characteristics they think are appropriate. **Assess** by having students draw up their own list.

Self-respect everywhere (Dotson & Dotson, 1997). Brainstorm with the class all of the different ways in which self-respect is played out in school, at home, in society, etc. What are some ways in which we show respect for ourselves? What implications does it have for the choices we make?

The relationship between diet and self-respect. Show students the Food Pyramid and discuss the relationship between food choices and self-respect. Talk about the eating disorders of anorexia and bulimia. How do these show a lack of self-respect? Discuss the physical consequences of these illnesses.

The links between self-respect and respecting others. After defining self-respect, facilitate a conversation among the class about the links between respecting self and respecting others. Is one who does well at one likely to be good at the other? Can one who fails to respect others really respect oneself?

Who are role models for respecting self (Dotson & Dotson, 1997)? Discuss with the class those who are role models for self-respect. Who in their world is particularly good at caring for themselves without being selfish? Who seems to value their own contributions while still valuing the contributions of others?

Who am I? Have students talk to their elders about the following questions: (1) How do I know I am normal? What is normal? (2) How does one determine one's sexuality? Are there symptoms? Is it a decision or a natural "given?" Are you stuck with it or is there a choice? (3) Why do I feel scared and confused about becoming an adult? (4) What does it mean to accept that this is my life and I have responsibility for it?

Developing Integrity by Building Your Identity

Ideas for Developing Skills

Level 3: Practice Procedures

Set goals, Plan steps of problem solving, Practice skills

Ethical role model. Students complete a survey regarding someone they consider their hero. "What makes a person a hero" is discussed after the survey is completed. Discussion should focus on whether the hero is someone whom exemplifies ethical behavior or is simply someone who looks "cool." Discussion can be facilitated by having the students describe the personality of their hero and imagine how their hero would act in a hypothetical situation.

Taking the perspective of people of honor. Students find situations about honor in films or stories and present them to the class. Of particular interest are stories and situations where characters sacrificed for society or someone other than a family member. Students can either elaborate on the text by writing a continuation or tangent to the story (related to helping behavior) or present the story to the class, or group, by acting out one or more roles of the characters involved in a sequence related to helping others.

Brainstorming values. Brainstorm with the class about what they perceive to be the most important values in our society. How does society collectively agree on them? How do we determine the action most consistent with the highest moral standard or public good?

Prepare a self-profile sheet (Dotson & Dotson, 1997). Prepare a self-profile sheet for students to complete. Ask them to list three each of the following: qualities they like best in themselves, qualities they think their teachers like, qualities their friends like, qualities that would make them good employees, qualities that their parents like, and hobbies or activities they enjoy and do well.

What describes you? Ask students to bring to class a sack of small items that describe themselves. As teacher, model the activity by introducing yourself using the items you selected, and then have each person say something about themselves related to their items.

Respecting self by clarifying and maintaining values. On a sheet of paper, have students list ten qualities that you especially admire and respect in a person. When finished, have them join with two or three other people to share their lists and identify the qualities that they listed in common. **Assess** by having the small groups present their three key values to the whole class.

Developing Integrity by Building Your Identity

Ideas for Developing Skills

Level 3 (continued)

Write an essay about yourself (Dotson & Dotson, 1997). Have the students write a personal essay in which they start every sentence with, "I like myself because..." Have them focus on their own personality, skills and abilities, more than external realities.

How can I be a role model for respecting self (Dotson & Dotson, 1997)? Discuss with the class those who are role models for self-respect and how each of them can become such a role model. What can they do to be better at caring for themselves without being selfish? How can they value their own contributions while still valuing the contributions of others?

Essay on identity. Students write an essay about their positive (ethical) identity and show it to an admired adult in the community who discusses the essay with the student. The student answers questions such as: What goals do I have for my life? What do I want people to say about me after I die? What kind of mark do I want to leave on the world? Whose life do I want to emulate?

Questions only I can answer. Write an essay about yourself. Begin the sentences in the following way: (1) I am, I want to be, I will be; (2) I think, I want to think, I will think; (3) I know, I want to know, I will know; (4) I wish, I want to wish, I will wish; (5) I feel, I want to feel, I will feel; (6) I wonder; (7) I see, I want to see, I will see; (8) I believe, I want to believe, I will believe; (9) I can; (10) I will. Discuss your essay with an adult mentor.

Level 4: Integrate Knowledge and Procedures

Execute plans, Solve problems

Choosing a positive identity. Have students identify specific skills and characteristics they would like to develop. Have them develop a set of steps for each goal and begin to implement the steps. Point out that identity and personal development is slow and takes time.

Develop a personal moral narrative. Have students write their life story, retrospectively and/or prospectively. Have them focus on the moral goals they have for their life, their actions, reasons for actions, accomplishments.

Starred ★ activities within each subskill go together!

Build Your Identity

Essays or Oral Reports. Have students write an essay or give an oral report about what they've learned about the importance of building an identity.

Interview. Assess an interview by having the students report back to the class, either in a written report or orally, what they talked about and learned from the interview.

Create a Self-Profile. Have students record observations of the qualities that they like best about themselves and the qualities that others may like best about them.

Individual Performance. Following a cooperative or class activity targeting an issue related to creating an identity, assess students on their individual contribution and performance.

Journaling. Over a period of time, have students record observations of their choices regarding personal health and self-care.

Developing Integrity by Reaching for Your Potential

Creative and Expert Implementer Real-life Example

Tiger Woods, Steven Spielberg, and ***Bob Dylan*** are each examples of those who have reached their potential in their chosen careers. Each one worked hard day in and day out, pushing themselves towards their dreams.

Ideas for Developing Skills

Level 1: Immersion in Examples and Opportunities

Attend to the big picture, Learn to recognize basic patterns

Stories of success. Read stories of those who worked hard and reached their goals (using stories from a book like *Unstoppable,* Kersey, 1998). Discuss what kept them going (their ideals and goals).

People at the top of their game. Identify and discuss individuals who have developed their talents to the fullest. Brainstorm about what they might have done to reach their fullest potential.

Human potential. In what ways do humans excel? (1) Students interview older students and adults about their opinions about human potential. What positive things do they strive for? What role models do they admire? (2) Have the students write up a report detailing their findings.

The future. Have students interview several different ages asking them to discuss what kind of world they would like to live in. How should people behave towards one another? What should people spend their time doing? What kinds of community event should there be? What kind of person (personal characteristics) do they want to be?

Level 2: Attention to Facts and Skills

Focus on detail and prototypical examples, Build knowledge

My future. Use questions from the interviews on other people's perceptions of the future and ask students to answer the same questions themselves. Have the students compare their answers with the interviewees and with each others. Emphasize the positive. After compiling a list (or the students making their own lists), the students write about the steps needed to reach one of their goals.

Starred activities within each subskill go together!

Developing Integrity by Reaching for Your Potential
Ideas for Developing Skills

Level 2 (continued)

Community stories. (a) Students gather stories of "best selves" from the community. Best selves refers to nurturing and displaying one's talents, positive spirit, and concern for the common good. Tape record them and then write them into a coherent story. (b) Compare and contrast the best selves stories from the community, discussing the themes to behaving your best.

Advantages of reaching your potential. Ask students to identify the advantages of reaching your potential. How do they benefit? What are some of the areas that need attention for them to reach their full potential?

Consider the people in your life who appear to have reached their potential. Have each student make a list of the people in their lives whom they think have reached their potential. Why would they describe them as such? How do they feel about those people? What most impresses the students about them? Assess by having the students report the person whom her or she thinks has best reached his or her potential.

Level 3: Practice Procedures
Set goals, Plan steps of problem-solving, Practice skills

Who do you want to be (Dotson & Dotson, 1997)? Ask students to draw a picture of themselves when they finish high school. In this drawing they should represent what kind of job they want to have, what their goals are for the future, what they will have already accomplished, and what their long-term dreams are.

Interview and report on professions of interest. Have the students interview someone who is in a profession that the student might wish to pursue. **Assess** with a report that outlines the necessary education and training to achieve that goal.

Making and keeping goals (Dotson & Dotson, 1997). Have students make a list of two goals for the week and five goals for the school year. Have them keep track of how they are doing in reaching their goals. **Assess** by collecting the papers and write an encouraging note to each student.

Teamwork project. Break up the class into teams and give each a specific task to complete (i.e., create a poster, collect newspaper articles, etc.) which portrays attempts at reaching one's potential. The goal is to complete the task while involving each person in the effort.

Starred activities within each subskill go together!

Developing Integrity by Reaching for Your Potential

Ideas for Developing Skills

Level 3 (continued)

Self-actualization. Maslow (1943) presented a set of characteristics that people have who are in the process of reaching their full potential. For the list of characteristics, see: http://mentalhelp.net/psyhelp/chap9/chap9g.htm. (1) Have students look for examples of people who have these characteristics. (2) Have students set a goal to work on one of the characteristics.

Level 4: Integrate Knowledge and Procedures

Execute plans, Solve problems

Mentor role-model. Have students identify their goals. Then pair them with a successful community member that can relate to their goals. Set up several activities for the pairs to do.

Reaching goals. Have students lay out specific goals and the strategies to reach them. Have them implement the strategies and report on progress. It would be helpful if an adult mentor could coach them (and evaluate their progress).

My Eulogy. Have students write about how they want to be remembered at the end of their life. What would they like someone to say about their life? The teacher can provide specific statements for the students to complete as part of this process (e.g., Xxx was a ________ person. Xxx always________. Xxx was very good at ______________. You could count on xxx to ________. Many people remember xxx for ______________ and _________. Xxx's ________, __________, and ________ will be sorely missed. Xxx made the world a better place by __________. Xxx's legacy is __________. Xxx's lasting achievements were ____________.) Ask students to take each statement and identify the characteristics and actions that would need to be exhibited (by them) to draw the conclusion. Have students set up goals based on what they describe. Have them break the goals into steps and begin to take the steps necessary to reach at least one of the goals. Report on progress.

Assessment Hints

Reach for Your Potential

Essays or Oral Reports. Have students write an essay or give an oral report about what they've learned about the importance of reaching their potential and who is a good exemplar of it in their lives.

Creative Writing. Have the students write a story that portrays someone who lives this skill particularly well.

Interview. Assess an interview by having the students report back to the class, either in a written report or orally, what they talked about and learned from the interview.

Journaling. Over a period of time, have students record observations of their own attempts at reaching their potential, and how well they are accomplishing it.

Group Project. Have the students break up into small groups to create a presentation for the class on the various ways that one might attempt to reach one's full potential.

Create a Climate
to Develop Ethical Identity and Integrity

- Emphasize the positive or negative impact an individual can have on others.
- Build lessons around transcendental themes (e.g., world peace, fighting hunger).
- Encourage students to think about their ideals and plans to reach them.
- Encourage students to talk to others about their ideal ethical identity and its impact on making a better world.
- Ascribe students' prosocial behavior to their intrinsic motivation as much as possible.
- Teach about the ways that individuals and groups influence the political process and make changes in society.
- Teach structures and strategies.
- Encourage independent thought and collaborative teamwork.
- Develop in students:
  Sense of self as an efficacious good person
  Sense of purpose
  Positive view
  Self actualization
- Make it clear that you expect students to nurture goodness in themselves and others.

Sample Student Self-Monitoring

Developing Ethical Identity and Integrity

Encourage active learning by having students learn to monitor their own learning

Choose Good Values

I know what are good choices and behaviors.
I want to choose what is good.
I want to foster good things in the world.
I know how to decide whether or not a choice is a good one.

Build Your Identity

I ask myself questions about who I should be.
I remember how other people have answered this question.
I compare the different ways people answer this question.

Reach for Your Potential

I set goals for myself.
I value honor in terms of self sacrifice, not in terms of hurting others.
I choose positive values out of respect for myself.
I live by my values.

Ethical Motivation Appendix

Lesson Planning Guide

'Linking to the Community' Worksheet

Rubric Examples

- Journaling
- Papers or Reports
- Group Project

Special Activities

- Cognitive Apprenticeship
- Cooperative Learning
- Guidelines for Cross-Age Tutoring
- Reciprocal Teaching
- The Jigsaw Method
- Structured Controversy

Making a Strategic Plan for Change

Linking EM Skills to Search Institute Assets

Recommended Resources for Character Education

Resources/References for Ethical Motivation

Lesson Planning Guide

1. Select an ethical category and identify the subskill you will address in your lesson(s).

2. Select a graduation standard or academic requirement and identify the sub-components.

3. Match up the ethical sub-skill with the academic sub-components.

4. Generate lesson activities using these elements:

(a) Enlist the communities resources.
(For ideas, consult the Linking to Community worksheet, pp. 158-163)

(b) Focus on a variety of teaching styles and intelligences.
Teaching styles: Visual, Auditory, Tactile, Kinesthetic, Oral, Individual/Cooperative, Olfactory, Gustatory, Spatial

Intelligences: Musical, Bodily-Kinesthetic, Spatial Logico-Mathematical, Linguistic, Interpersonal, Intrapersonal

(c) Identify questions that you can ask that promote different kinds of thinking and memory.

Creative Thinking

Prospective Thinking

Retrospective Thinking

Motivational Thinking

Practical Thinking

Types of Memory:

Autobiographical (personal experience)

Narrative (storyline)

Procedural (how to)

Semantic (what)

5. Create an activity for each <u>level of expertise</u> you will address (worksheet provided on next page). Indicate which activities fit with which lesson. For each activity, indicate how you will <u>assess learning</u>.

Lesson Planning Guide
(continued)

ACTIVITY STUDENT ASSESSMENT

Level 1: Immersion in Examples and Opportunities
(Attend to the big picture, Learn to recognize basic patterns)

Level 2: Attention to Facts and Skills
(Focus on detail and prototypical examples, Build knowledge)

Level 3: Practice Procedures
(Set goals, Plan steps of problem solving, Practice skills)

Level 4: Integrate Knowledge and Procedures
(Execute plans, Solve problems)

CHECKLIST FOR

Linking to the Community

What resources must be accessed for learning the skill or subskill?

What resources must be identified to successfully complete the skill or subskill?

1. SOCIAL NETWORK RESOURCES

Circle the resources that must be accessed for learning the skill:

Family___ Friendship___ Service group___

Neighborhood___ Social groups ___ Community___

City___ Park & Rec___ State___

National ___ International___

Other:________________________ Other:________________________

On the line next to each circled item, indicate the manner of contact:

Contact in person (P), by telephone (T)

2. SEMANTIC KNOWLEDGE RESOURCES

Circle the resources that must be accessed for learning the skill:

Books and other library sources___ Web___

Librarians___ Educators and Intellectuals___

Business leaders___ Community experts___

Other:________________________ Other:________________________

On the line next to each circled item, indicate the manner of contact:

Contact in person (P), Email (E), Web (W), Letter (L), Telephone (T)

CHECKLIST FOR
Linking to the Community
(continued)

3. AUTHORITY STRUCTURE RESOURCES

Circle the resources that must be accessed for learning the skill:

School officials___ Government officials (all levels) ___ United Nations___

Other Leaders:____

____

____

Indicate the manner of contact for each item:

Contact in person (P), Telephone (T), Letter (L), Email (E)

4. ORGANIZATIONAL RESOURCES

What types of organizations can give guidance?

____

____

____

____

How can they help?

____

____

____

____

____

____

____

____

CHECKLIST FOR
Linking to the Community
(continued)

5. **AGE GROUP RESOURCES**

Circle the resources that must be accessed for learning the skill:

- Teen groups in various community organizations_____

  Specify:

- School groups_____

  Specify:

- Senior citizen groups_____

  Specify:

- Children's groups_____

  Specify:

- Women's groups_____

  Specify:

- Men's groups_____

  Specify:

Indicate the manner of contact for each circled item:

Contact in person (P), Telephone (T), Letter (L), Email (E)

CHECKLIST FOR
Linking to the Community
(continued)

6. MATERIAL RESOURCES

Types of Materials

- scraps (from scrap yards)
- second-hand (from second-hand stores, recycling places)
- new
- handmade

Identify the resources that must be accessed for learning the skill:

What materials do you need for your project?

____

____

____

Where can you get it?

____

____

____

How can you get it?

____

____

____

Indicate the manner of contact for each item:

Contact in person (P), Telephone (T), Letter (L), Email (E)

CHECKLIST FOR Linking to the Community (continued)

7. EXPERTISE RESOURCES

Types of Expertise

social networking _____ design_____ musical _____

physical (game/sport, dance) _____ creating_____ knowledge _____

finance_____ selling _____

Identify the resources that must be accessed for learning the skill:

What expertise is required?

____

____

____

____

Who has expertise?

____

____

____

Can I develop expertise or must I depend on an expert?

____

____

Who can help me figure out what to do?

____

____

____

Indicate the manner of contact for each item:

Telephone (T), Take a class (C), Contact in person (P), Book (B)

CHECKLIST FOR
Linking to the Community
(continued)

8. FINANCIAL RESOURCES

Circle the sources that must be accessed for learning the skill:

Grants___ Loans___ Donors___

Earn money___

Bartering (use library and experts to find these out) ___

Indicate the manner of contact for each circled item:

Contact in person (P), Telephone (T), Letter (L), Email (E)

9. PERSONAL RESOURCES

What abilities and skills do I have that I can use to reach the goal?

____

____

____

____

10. OTHER RESOURCES

What other resources might be needed or are optional?

____

____

____

____

Rubric Examples

GUIDES FOR CREATING YOUR OWN RUBRIC

Creating Rubrics
(Blueprint of behavior for peak or acceptable level of performance)

- Establish Learner Outcome goals
- Cluster these characteristics
- Determine which combinations of characteristics show Unsatisfactory, Satisfactory, Excellent 'job'
- Create examples of work showing different levels of performance
- List expectations on a form
- Present criteria to students ahead of time

RUBRIC FOR JOURNALING

Quality of Journaling		
Content: Quantity Few requirements for content are covered. 0 1 2 3	Most requirements are included fairly well. 4 5 6 7	Content requirements are thoroughly covered. 8 9 10
Content: Type Rarely are both feelings and thoughts included in entries. 0 1 2 3	Sometimes both feelings and thoughts are included in entries. 4 5 6 7	Both feelings and thoughts are included in entries. 8 9 10
Content: Clarity Entries are difficult to understand. 0 1 2 3	Entries can be understood with some effort. 4 5 6 7	Entries are easily understood. 8 9 10

Rubric Examples (continued)

RUBRIC FOR PAPERS OR REPORTS

Qualities of Paper or Written Report		
Organization The paper is difficult to follow. 0 1 2 3	The paper is easy to follow and read. 4 5 6 7	All relationships among ideas are clearly expressed by the sentence structures and word choices. 8 9 10
Writing Style The style of the writing is sloppy, has no clear direction, looks like it was written by several people. 0 1 2 3	The format is appropriate with correct spelling, good grammar, good punctuation and appropriate transition sentences. 4 5 6 7	The paper is well written and is appropriate for presentation in the firm. 8 9 10
Content The paper has no point. The ideas are aimless, disconnected. 0 1 2 3	The paper makes a couple of clear points but weakly, with few supportive facts. 4 5 6 7	The paper makes one or two strong points. Support for these arguments is well described. 8 9 10

Rubric Examples (continued)

RUBRIC FOR GROUP PROJECT

(Bloomer & Lutz as cited in Walvoord & Anderson, 1998)

Evaluation of a Group Project*	Rating
Comprehension: Seemed to understand requirements for assignment.	0 1 2 3 Not Observed
Problem Identification and Solution: Participated in identifying and defining problems and working towards a solution.	0 1 2 3 Not Observed
Organization: Approached tasks (such as time management) in systematic way.	0 1 2 3 Not Observed
Acceptance of responsibility: Took responsibility for assigned tasks in the project.	0 1 2 3 Not Observed
Initiative/motivation: Made suggestions, sought feedback, showed interest in group decision making and planning.	0 1 2 3 Not Observed
Creativity: Considered ideas from unusual or different viewpoints.	0 1 2 3 Not Observed
Task completion: Followed through in completing own contributions to the group project.	0 1 2 3 Not Observed
Attendance: Attended planning sessions, was prompt and participated in decision making.	0 1 2 3 Not Observed

Add Total Score — Total:______________

Divide by number of items scored with a number — Average:___________

Comments:

Special Activities

COGNITIVE APPRENTICESHIP

(Collins, Hawkins, & Carver, 1991, p. 228)

Teach *process* (how to) and *provide guided experience* in cognitive skills.

Teach *content* relevant to the task.

Teach this content for each subject area:

- Strategic knowledge: how to work successfully in the subject area
- Domain knowledge: the kind of knowledge experts know
- Problem solving strategies particular to the subject area

Learning strategies for the subject area

Teaching methods to use:

- Expert modeling
- Coaching
- Scaffolding (lots of structured assistance at first, gradual withdrawal of support)
- Articulation by students
- Reflection
- Exploration

How to sequence material:

- Increasing complexity
- Increasing diversity
- Global (the big picture) before the local (the detail)

Learning environment should emphasize:

- Situated learning
- Community of practice
- Intrinsic motivation
- Cooperation

COOPERATIVE LEARNING

Necessary elements in using cooperative learning to improve role-taking (Bridgeman, 1981)

1. Required interdependence and social reciprocity
2. Consistent opportunity to be an expert
3. Integration of varied perspectives and appreciation for the result
4. Equal status cooperation
5. Highly structured to allow easy replication of these interactions

Special Activities

GUILDELINES FOR CROSS-GRADE TUTORING

(Heath & Mangiola, 1991)

1. Allow a preparation period of at least 1 month to 6 weeks for the student tutors.
2. Use as much writing as possible in the context of the tutoring from the very beginning. Use a variety of sources and use the tutoring as a basis for tutors to write to different audiences.
3. Make field notes meaningful as a basis for conversation by providing students with occasions to share their notes orally.
4. Provide students with supportive models of open-ended questioning.
5. Emphasize the ways in which tutors can extend tutees' responses and elicit elaboration from tutees in order to impress upon them the importance of talk in learning.
6. Discuss the ways the topic relates to students' experiences.
7. Provide opportunities for tutors to prepare.
8. Develop real audiences for the students' work.

RECIPROCAL TEACHING (RT)

Context	One-on-one in laboratory settings	Groups in resource rooms	Naturally occurring groups in classrooms	Work groups fully integrated into science classrooms
Activities	Summarizing, questioning, clarifying, predicting	Gist and analogy	Complex argument structure	Thought experiments
Materials	Unconnected passages	Coherent content	Research-related resources material	Student-prepared
Pattern of use	Individual strategy training	Group discussion	Planned RT for learning content and jigsaw teaching	Opportunistic use of RT

Special Activities

THE JIGSAW METHOD

(Aronson & Patnoe, 1997)

The Jigsaw Method of cooperative learning helps children work together on an equal basis. It has been shown to improve empathy for fellow students, mastery of course material, liking of school and liking of classmates.

Goal: That students treat each other as resources
Instructional outcome: Students learn that it is possible to work together without sacrificing excellence.
Structure:

Individual competition is incompatible with success.
Success is dependent on cooperative behavior.
All students has unique information to bring to the group.

You must provide material written by relative experts. This could be an article broken into pieces or could be cards on which you write critical information.

1. Divide the written material into 3-6 coherent parts (could be by paragraphs).
2. Assign students to 3-5 groups.
3. Assign one part of the material to each group member.
4. Those with the same part meet in groups to learn their knowledge (10-15 minutes).
5. Group members return to their original groups to learn from their group.
6. Everyone takes a quiz on all the material.

STRUCTURED CONTROVERSY

The steps for a structured academic controversy (Johnson & Johnson, 1997) are as follows:

(1) Select an issue relevant to what you are studying. Select two or more opinions on the issue.

(2) Form advocacy teams by putting the students into groups for each different opinion. Either put together a list of supporting statements for each opinion, or have students research the opinion and come up with their own supporting statements (if this is done, provide guidance and feedback for the accuracy and comprehensiveness of the supporting statements they generate). Each group prepares a persuasive statement based on the supporting statements of their opinion.

(3) Have each group present its persuasive case to the other groups without interruption. Students in the listening groups should listen carefully and take notes to learn the other opinion well.

(4) Have open discussion among the groups with advocacy of their own position and refutation of other positions (respectfully).

(5) Groups trade positions on the issue to take another group's perspective. The group must present the other perspective to the others as sincerely and persuasively as the original group did. The group can add new facts, information, or arguments to the position (based on what they have already learned) to make it more persuasive.

(6) All individuals drop their advocacy and group-orientation to discuss the positions again and try to come to a consensus about which position is the best. The position can be one that is a synthesis of two or more, as long as the position isn't a simple compromise.

Special Activities

STRUCTURED CONTROVERSY
LESSON PLANNING SHEET

Grade Level_________ Subject area_________________________

Size of group_______ How groups formed___________________

Room arrangement_________________________

Issue____

One perspective_____________________________________

Second perspective___________________________________

Third perspective____________________________________

Student materials required_____________________________________

Define the controversy____

____

____

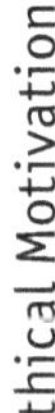

Making a strategic plan for change

1. **What I/we want to change:**

2. **The end result I/we want:**

3. **What is current reality—now?** Identify the difference between where things stand now and where you want to get to.

4. **What steps do I/we need to take to get to the desired end result?** Brainstorm on methods or strategies to reach your objectives. Don't eliminate any methods or strategies at this point.

5. **How will I/we know my/our actions are working?** Brainstorm on ways to check that actions are or are not working.

6. **Now select the best goals and the best set of steps to reach them.** Make sure:

- That the goals are going to reach the end result we desire. (Imagine the strategies successfully completed.)
- To quantify the goal where you can.
- To translate comparative terms (e.g., more, better, less, increased) into their actual goals.
- To create long-term, lasting results rather than just solving individual problems.
- That your goals describe an actual result rather than only a process for achieving that result.
- That your goals are specific.

Linking EJ Skills to Search Institute Assets

VIRTUE / SUBSKILL	EM-1 Respecting Others	EM-2 Cultivating Conscience	EM-3 Acting Responsibly	EM-4 Helping Others	EM-5 Finding Meaning	EM-6 Valuing Traditions	EM-7 Ethical Identity
1. Family support			*	*		*	
2. Positive family comm.							
3. Other adult relationships	*					*	
4. Caring neighborhood			*	*		*	
5. Caring school climate	*	*	*	*		*	*
6. Parent involvement in school							
7. Community values youth			*				*
8. Youth as resources	*	*	*	*		*	*
9. Service to others			*				
10. Safety				*			*
11. Family boundaries	*	*	*				
12. School boundaries			*				
13. Neighborhood boundaries			*				
14. Adult role models	*	*	*	*	*	*	*
15. Positive peer influence	*		*	*	*		*
16. High expectations							*
17. Creative activities					*		
18. Youth programs					*		
19. Religious community	*	*		*	*		*
20. Time at home				*			*
21. Achievement motivation					*		
22. School engagement							
23. Homework	*	*	*	*	*		*
24. Bonding to school							*
25. Reading for pleasure	*	*	*	*			*
26. Caring	*	*	*	*	*		*
27. Equality and social justice	*	*	*	*			*
28. Integrity							
29. Honesty	*	*	*	*			*
30. Responsibility	*	*	*		*		*
31. Restraint		*		*	*		
32. Planning and decision making	*	*		*	*		
33. Interpersonal competence							
34. Cultural competence		*					
35. Resistance skills							
36. Peaceful conflict resolution		*	*	*	*		*
37. Personal power		*		*	*		*
38. Self-esteem			*	*			*
39. Sense of purpose					*		
40. Positive view of personal future					*		

Recommended Resources for Character Education

Alberti, R. E., & Emmons, M. L. (1974). *Your perfect right: A guide to assertive behavior.* San Luis Obispo, CA: Impact.

Alliance for Service-Learning in Education Reform. (1995). *Standards of quality for school-based and community-based service learning.* National Service-Learning Clearinghouse.

Anderson, R.C. (1977). The notion of schemata and the educational enterprise. In R.C. Anderson & R. Spiro (Eds.), *Schooling and the acquisition of knowledge.* Hillsdale, NJ: Erlbaum.

Anderson, R. C. (1984), Role of readers schema in comprehension, learning, and memory. In R. C. Anderson, J. Osborn, & R. J. Tierney (Eds.), *Learning to read in American schools: Basal readers and content texts.* Hillsdale, NJ: Erlbaum.

Archambault, R. (1964). (Ed.). *John Dewey on education.* New York: Random House.

Babbitt, I. (1919). *Rousseau and romanticism.* Boston: Houghton Mifflin.

Banks, J. A., & Banks, C. A. (1997). *Multicultural education: Issues and perspectives.* New York: Allyn & Bacon.

Banks, J.A. (1988). *Multiethnic education.* New York: Allyn & Bacon.

Bargh, J. (1989). Conditional automaticity: Varieties of automatic influence in social perception and cognition. In J. Uleman & J. Bargh (Eds.), *Unintended thought.* New York: Guilford.

Bebeau, M., Rest, J. R., & Narvaez, D. (1999). Beyond the promise: A framework for research in moral education. *Educational Researcher, 28*(4), 18-26.

Bellah, R. N., Madsen, R., Sullivan, W. M., Swindler, A., & Tipton, S. M. (1985). *Habits of the heart: Individualism and commitment in American life.* Berkeley: University of California Press.

Bennett, C. I. (1990). *Comprehensive multicultural education.* Boston: Allyn & Bacon.

Bergem, T. (1990). The teacher as moral agent. *Journal of Ethical Education, 19*(2), 88-100.

Berliner, D. C., & Biddle, B. J. (1995). *The manufactured crisis: Myths, fraud and the attack on America's public schools.* New York: Addison-Wesley.

Berman, S. (1997). *Children's social consciousness and the development of social responsibility.* Albany: State University of New York Press.

Blasi, A. (1984). Moral identity: Its role in moral functioning. In W. M. Kurtines & J. L. Gewirtz (Eds.), *Morality, moral behavior, and moral development* (pp. 128-139). New York: Wiley-Interscience.

Bloom, A. (1987). *The closing of the American mind.* New York: Simon & Schuster.

Bransford, J. D., & Stein, B. S. (1984). *The ideal problem solver.* New York: Freeman.

Byrnes, D. A., & Kiger, G. (1996). *Common bonds: Anti-bias teaching in a diverse society.* New York: Association for Childhood Education.

Campbell, D. E. (1996). *Choosing democracy: A practical guide to multicultural education.* New York: Merrill. Greene, A. (1996). *Rights to responsibility: Multiple approaches to developing character and community.* Tucson, AZ: Zephyr.

Cromer, A. (1993). *Uncommon sense.* New York: Oxford University Press.

Csikszentmihalyi, M. (1993). *The evolving self.* New York: Harper and Collins.

Damon, W. (1984). Self-understanding and moral development from childhood to adolescence. In W. Kurtines & J. L. Gewirtz (Eds.), *Morality, moral behavior, and moral development* (pp. 109-127). New York: Wiley.

Damon, W. (1995). *Greater expectations: Overcoming the culture of indulgence in America's homes and schools.* New York: Free Press.

Diamond, B. J., & Moore, M. A. (1995). *Multicultural literacy: Mirroring the new reality of the classroom.* New York: Longman.

Diamond, J. (1997). *Guns, germs and steel: The fates of human societies.* New York: W.W. Norton.

De Vries, R., & Zan, B. S. (1994). *Moral classrooms, moral children: Creating a constructivist atmosphere in early education.* New York: Teachers College Press.

Ehman, L. H. (1980). The American school in the political socialization process. *Review of Educational Research, 50*(1), 99-102.

Elias, M. J., Arnold, H., & Hussey, C. S. (Eds.). (2002). *EQ + IQ = Best leadership practices for caring and successful schools.* Thousand Oaks, CA: Corwin Press

Eisenberg, N., & Mussen, P.H. (1995). *The roots of prosocial behavior in children.* Cambridge, MA: Cambridge University Press.

Ennis, R. H. (1987). A taxonomy of critical thinking dispositions and abilities. In J. Baron & R. Sternberg (Eds.), *Teaching thinking skills: Theory and practice*. New York: Freeman.

Etzioni, A. (1993). *The spirit of community*. New York: Crown.

Fisher, R., & Ury, W. (1981). *Getting to yes: Negotiating agreement without giving in*. London: Penguin.

Freedman, G., & Reynolds, E. G. (1980). Enriched basic reader lessons with semantic webbing. *Reading Teachers, 33*, 677-683.

Gazzaniga, M. S., Ivry, R. B., & Mangun, G. R. (1998). *Cognitive neuroscience: The biology of the mind*. New York: Norton.

Glazer, N. (1997). *We are all multiculturalists now*. Cambridge, MA: Harvard University Press.

Gollnick, D.M., & Chinn, P.C. (1994). *Multicultural education in a pluralistic society*. New York: Merrill.

Goodlad, J., Soder, R., & Sirotnik, K. (1990). *The moral dimensions of teaching*. San Francisco: Jossey-Bass.

Gootman, M. E. (2008). *The caring teacher's guide to discipline: Helping students learn self-control, responsibility, and respect, K-6* (3rd ed.). Thousand Oaks, CA: Corwin Press.

Grant, C. A., & Sleeter, C. E. (1997). *Turning on learning: Five approaches for multicultural plans for race, class, gender, and disability*. New York: Prentice Hall.

Greene, A. (1996). *Rights to responsibility: Multiple approaches to developing character and community*. Tucson, AZ: Zephyr.

Jenning, T. E. (1992). *Self-in-connection as a component of human rights advocacy*. Unpublished manuscript.

Jweid, R., & Rizzo, M. (2001). *Building character through literature: A guide for middle school readers*. Lanham, MD: Scarecrow.

Kabagarama, D. (1997). *Breaking the ice: A guide to understanding people from other cultures* (2nd ed.). New York: Prentice Hall.

Kelso, W. A. (1994). *Poverty and the underclass*. New York: New York University Press.

Kinsley, L. (1992). *Case study: The integration of community service in the curriculum by an interdisciplinary team*. St. Paul: NSLCC Library, University of Minnesota at St. Paul.

Kirschenbaum, H. (1994). *100 ways to enhance values and morality in schools and youth meetings*. Boston: Allyn & Bacon.

Kohlberg, L. (1984). *The psychology of moral development*. New York: Harper & Row.

Kozol, J. (1991). *Savage inequalities*. New York: Harper Collins.

Kurtzman, L. (1998, October). *Advertising play*. Paper presented at the meeting of the Character Education Partnership, Denver, CA.

Kurtzman, L. (1998, October). *Peer leaders: Cross-age Grade 7 and 6 to Grade 4 and 3*. Paper presented at the meeting of the Character Education Partnership, Denver, CA.

La Belle, T. J., & Ward, C. R. (1994). *Multiculturalism and education*. Albany: State University of New York.

Ladson-Billings, G. (1991). *The dreamkeepers: Successful teachers of African-American children*. New York: Jossey-Bass.

Lantieri, L., & Goleman, D. (2008). *Building emotional intelligence: Techniques to cultivate inner strength in children*. Boulder, CO: Sounds True, Incorporated.

Liebling, C. R. (1986). *Inside view and character plans in original stories and their basal reader adaptations*. Washington, DC: National Institute of Education.

Lozanov, G. (1978). *Suggestology and outlines of suggestopedy*. New York: Gordon and Breach.

Markus, H. R., & Kitayama, S. (1991). Culture and self: Implications for cognition, emotion, and motivation. *Psychological Bulletin, 98*, 224-253.

Marzano, R. J., Brandt, R. S., Hughes, C. S., Jones, B. F., Presseisen, B. Z., Rankin, S. C., & Suhor, C. (1988). *Dimensions of thinking: A framework for curriculum and instruction*. Alexandria, VA: Association for Supervision and Curriculum Development.

Means, B., Chelemer, C., & Knapp, M. S. (1991). *Teaching advanced skills to at-risk students*. San Francisco: Jossey Bass.

Melchior, A. (1997). *National Evaluation of Learn and Serve America School and Community-Based Programs: Interim Report*. New York: The Corporation for National Service.

Miller, J. C., & Clarke, C. (1998). *10-minute life lessons for kids: 52 fun and simple games and activities to teach your child trust, honesty, love, and other important values*. New York: HarperPerennial Library.

Molnar, A. (1997). *The construction of children's character*. Chicago: University of Chicago Press.

Narvaez, D. (1996, November). *Moral perception: A new construct?* Paper presented at the annual meeting of the American Educational Research Association, New York.

Narvaez, D. (1998). The effects of moral schemas on the reconstruction of moral narratives in 8th grade and college students. *Journal of Educational Psychology, 90*(1), 13-24.

Narvaez, D., Gleason, T., Mitchell, C., & Bentley, J. (1999). Moral theme comprehension in children. *Journal of Educational Psychology, 91*(3), 477-487.

Nieto, S. (1992). *Affirming diversity: The sociopolitical context of multicultural education*. New York: Longman.

Noddings, N. (1997). Character education and community. In A. Molnar (Ed.), *The construction of children's character* (pp. 1-16). Chicago: University of Chicago Press.

Nucci, L. P., & Narvaez, D. (Eds.). (2008). *Handbook of moral and character education*. New York: Routledge.

Perry, T., & Fraser, J. W. (1993). *Freedom's plow: Teaching in the multicultural classroom*. New York: Routledge.

Persell, C. H. (1997). *Education and inequality: A theoretical and empirical synthesis*. New York: Free Press.

Power, F. C., Nuzzi, R. J., Narvaez, D., Lapsley, D. K., & Hunt, T. C. (Eds.). (2008). *Moral education: A handbook* (Vols. 1-2). Westport, CT: Praeger.

Prothrow-Stith, D., & Weissman, M. (1991). *Deadly consequences: How violence is destroying our teenage population and a plan to begin solving the problem*. New York: Harper Perennial.

Purpel, D. (1997). The politics of character education. In A. Molnar (Ed.), *The construction of children's character* (pp. 140-153). Chicago: University of Chicago Press.

Reed, E., Turiel, E., & Brown, T. (1996). *Values and knowledge*. Mahwah, NJ: Lawrence Erlbaum Associates.

Rest, J. R. (1979). *Development in judging moral issues*. Minneapolis, MN: University of Minnesota Press.

Rest, J. R. (1983). Morality. In P. Mussen (Series Ed.), J. Flavell & E. Markham (Vol. Eds.), *Handbook of child psychology: Vol. 3. Cognitive development* (pp. 556-629). New York: Wiley.

Rest, J. R., & Narvaez, D. (1994). *Moral development in the professions: Psychology and applied ethics*. Hillsdale, NJ: Lawrence Erlbaum.

Rumelhart, D. (1975). Notes on a schema for stories. In D. Bobrow & A. Collins (Eds.), *Representation and understanding: Studies in cognitive science*. New York: Academic Press.

Ryan, K. A., & Bohlin, K. E. (2000). *Building character in schools: Practical ways to bring moral instruction to life*. San Francisco: Jossey-Bass.

Ryan, K., & Wynne, E. A. (1996). *Reclaiming our schools: Teaching character, academics, and discipline*. Upper Saddle River, NJ: Prentice Hall.

Schacter, D. (1996). *Searching for memory*. New York: Basic Books.

Schaps, E., Battistich, V., & Solomon, D. (1997). School as a caring community: A key to character education. In A. Molnar (Ed.), *The construction of children's character* (pp. 127-139). Chicago: University of Chicago Press.

Schlaefli, A., Rest, J., & Thoma, S. (1985). Does moral education improve moral judgment? A Meat-analysis of intervention studies using the Defining Issues Test. *Review of Educational Research, 55*(3), 319-352.

Schorr, L.A. (1988). *Within our reach: Breaking the cycle of disadvantage*. New York: Anchor.

Schubert, W.H. (1997). Character education from four perspectives on curriculum. In A. Molnar (Ed.), *The construction of children's character* (pp. 17-30). Chicago: University of Chicago Press.

Sleeter, C. E., & Grant, C. A. (1998). *Making choices for multicultural education: Five approaches to race, class, and gender*. New York: MacMillan.

Sowell, T. (1994). *Race and culture*. New York: Basic Books.

Sowell, T. (1996). *Migration and cultures*. New York: Basic Books.

Steinberg, L. (1996). *Beyond the classroom*. New York: Simon & Schuster.

Sternberg, R. (1998). Principles of teaching for successful intelligence. *Educational Psychologist, 33*(2-3), 65-72.

Sykes, C. J. (1992). *A nation of victims*. New York: St. Martin's Press.

Triandis, H. C. (1995). *Individualism and collectivism*. Boulder, CO: Westview Press.

Watson, M., & Eckert, L. (2003). *Learning to trust*. San Francisco: Jossey-Bass.

Wilson, W. J. (1996). *When work disappears: The world of the new urban poor*. New York: Alfred Knopf.

Wynne, E. A., & Ryan, K. (1993). *Reclaiming our schools: Teaching character; academics and discipline*. Upper Saddle River, NJ: Prentice Hall.

Wynne, E. A., & Ryan, K. (1996). *Reclaiming our schools* (2nd ed.). New York: Merrill.

Zajonc, R. B. (1980). Feeling and thinking: Preferences need no inferences. *American Psychologist, 35*, 151-175.

Resources/References for Ethical Motivation

ACADEMIC ACHIEVEMENT

The Efficacy Institute, Inc.
182 Felton Street
Waltham, MA 02453-4134
781.547.6060
781.547.6077 FAX
info@efficacy.org
http://www.efficacy.org/

Description: The Efficacy Institute works to release the intellectual capacity of all children, especially children of color, and to affirm their right to learn. Part of its mission is to help teachers and other adults learn that development is a learnable, teachable process that all of us are responsible for managing. The institute is committed to breaking the cycle of underdevelopment and eradicating the myth of genetic inferiority.

Minnesota Minority Education Partnership, Inc.
Wright Building
2233 University Ave West, Suite 220
St. Paul, MN 55114
www.mmep.net

Description: This guide was developed to assist youth in identifying summer academic programs which may help them prepare for post-secondary education. The Minnesota Minority Education Partnership (MMEP) is a collaborative effort committed to increasing the success of Minnesota students of color in Minnesota schools, colleges, and universities.

Resources/References for Ethical Motivation

CITIZENSHIP EDUCATION

Character Builder Web Site
http://www.uensd.org/USOE_Pages/ic/chared/default.html

Character Education Partnership
1025 Connecticut Ave NW, Suite 1011
Washington, DC 20036
www.character.org/search
Description: Character Education Partnership's (CEP) Online Database has character education resources and organizations, scroll through material from CEP's Character Education Resource Guide, or view a list of other character education web sites.

Civic Organizing, Inc.
http://www.activecitizen.org
Description: Civic Organizing, Inc. provides a list of recommended readings that are some key works associated with the history of democratic movements, as well as some current works on professional culture and education that have influenced the development of civic organizing.

National Council for the Social Studies
8555 Sixteenth Street, Suite 500
Silver Spring, MD 20910
301-588-1800
www.socialstudies.org
Description: The mission of National Council for the Social Studies (NCSS) is to provide leadership, service, and support for all social studies educators, who teach students the content knowledge, intellectual skills, and civic values necessary for fulfilling the duties of citizenship in a participatory democracy. NCSS offers teaching resources in many areas of social studies, including civic ideals and practices and power, authority, and governance.

U.S. House of Representatives/U.S. Senate web sites
www.house.gov OR www.senate.gov
Description: Students can learn about the U.S. House of Representatives by accessing this web site.

Resources/References for Ethical Motivation

CONFLICT RESOLUTION

Conflict Resolution Information Source
c/o Conflict Information Consortium
University of Colorado
Campus Box 580
Boulder CO 80309
http://www.crinfo.org/
Description: A staff of editors maintains a keyword-coded catalog of over 20,000 web, print, and organizational resources on conflict resolution.

Peacemaker! A Conflict Resolution Program for Youth—There is HOPE
National Service Resource Center
ETR Associates
4 Carbonero Way
Scotts Valley, CA 95066
http://www.nationalserviceresources.org/library/items/V0848
Description: This video (NIMCO, 1996) shows the making of a real-life situation video by teens to illustrate ways of dealing with conflict and avoiding violence. It includes interviews with students about their lives in a high-risk neighborhood.

Resources/References for Ethical Motivation

DRUG AND ALCOHOL PREVENTION

Project Charlie
6425 Nicollet Avenue S
Minneapolis, MN 55423-1668
(612) 861-1675

Description: Through curriculum and training, Project Charlie equips teachers with the skills and information they need to teach children social competencies that will lead them to choose not to use! Project Charlie programs include both school and home-based curriculum for prevention in drug abuse, physical and sexual abuse, and violence prevention for elementary and middle school age children.

ENVIRONMENTAL STEWARDSHIP

(cultivating a personal commitment to responsible resource management through knowing about and caring for the environment and applying this concern through responsible action)

Carolina Coastal Science web site
http://www.ncsu.edu/coast/
Description: The Carolina Coastal Science web site is an innovative, inquiry-based, science resource that explores science in coastal Carolina. While this Web site has been designed specifically for an Environmental Science component of an elementary, middle school, or upper secondary science curriculum, it may be used in different curricular areas.

Give Water a Hand web site
www.uwex.edu/erc/gwah
Description: With Give Water A Hand, young people team up with educators, natural resource experts and committed community members to study water issues and take ACTION! Students learn about Give Water a Hand and how they can launch this successful program in their own community or school through accessing this web site.

Resources/References for Ethical Motivation

U. S. Fish and Wildlife Service web site
www.fws.gov
Description: The mission of U.S. Fish and Wildlife Service is working with others to conserve, protect, and enhance fish, wildlife, and plants and their habitats for the continuing benefit of the American people. Students can learn about endangered species, environmental contaminants, fisheries, migratory birds, and waterfowl at this web site.

Ask a Geologist web site
http://walrus.wr.usgs.gov/docs/ask-a-ge.html
Description: Do students have questions about volcanoes, earthquakes, mountains, rocks, maps, ground water, lakes, or rivers? Students can email earth science questions to geologists. They answer about 45% of incoming messages. They encourage students to send in questions, but will not write reports or answer test questions for them.

PEACE BUILDING

These organizations can provide information on peace education:

Richmond Peace Education Center
400 W 32nd Street
Richmond VA 23225
804-232-1002
www.rpec.org

PeaceBuilders
PeacePartners, Inc.
741 Atlantic Ave.
Long Beach, CA 90813
www.peacebuilders.com

Peace Education Foundation
1900 Biscayne Blvd.
Miami FL 33132
305-576-5075
www.peace-ed.org

Resources/References for Ethical Motivation

PEER MEDIATION

These organizations can provide information on peer mediation and conflict resolution.

Cooperative Learning Center
University of Minnesota
http://www.co-operation.org/

Conflict Resolution/Peer Mediation Research
University of Florida
www.coe.ufl.edu/CRPM/CRPMhome.html

SERVICE LEARNING

National Service-Learning Clearinghouse
ETR Associates
4 Carbonero Way
Scotts Valley CA 95066
866-245-7378
http://www.servicelearning.org
Description: The Learn & Serve America National Service-Learning Clearinghouse is a comprehensive information system that focuses on all dimensions of service-learning, covering kindergarten through higher education school-based, as well as community-based initiatives. The center of the Clearinghouse is located at the University of Minnesota, Department of Work, Community and Family Education, with collaboration from a consortium of twelve other institutions and organizations.

Resources/References for Ethical Motivation

National Youth Leadership Council
1667 Snelling Ave North
Suite D300
St. Paul, MN 55108
651-631-3672
http://www.nylc.org/
Description: The National Youth Leadership Council's (NYLC) mission is to engage young people in their communities and schools through innovation in learning, service, leadership, and public policy. As one of America's most prominent advocates of service-learning and youth service, NYLC is at the forefront of efforts to reform education and guide youth-oriented public policy.

Resource Center
Corporation for National and Community Service
ETR Associates
4 Carbonero Way
Scotts Valley, CA 95066
http://www.nationalserviceresources.org/
Description: The National Service Resource Center offers manuals and guides for doing service learning, including *Essential Elements of Service Learning* (National Service Learning Cooperative, 1998), *Service-Learning: Linking Classrooms & Communities* (California Department of Education, 1999), and *Teens Volunteering: The Guide* (Dungca, 1998).

VOLUNTEERISM

Directory of Youth Volunteer Opportunities
United Way
www.liveunited.org

Resources/References for Ethical Motivation

PERIODICALS FOR PEACE AND NON-VIOLENCE

(list is mostly from Mark Shepherd, www.markshep.com)

The Acorn, a scholarly Gandhian journal from the U.S. (Box 107, St. Bonaventure, NY 14778; 716-375-2275; BGan@sbu.edu)

Communities Magazine, mostly about intentional, utopian communities, but can also have articles on cooperatives and other small-scale alternatives (138 Twin Oaks Rd, Louisa, VA 23093;communities@ic.org; communities.ic.org)

Fellowship Magazine, from the U.S. branch of the Fellowship of Reconciliation (Box 271, Nyack, NY 10960; 914-358-4601; Fellowship@forusa.org; www.forusa.org/fellowship)

Gandhi Magazine, a scholarly journal from the Gandhi Peace Foundation (221 Deen Dayal, Upadhyaya Marg, New Delhi 110 002 INDIA; +91-11-331-7491)

Non-Violence Today, an Australian journal (P.O. Box 5292, West End QLD 4101 AUSTRALIA; d.keenan@uq.net.au)

Peace Magazine, a Canadian journal, edited by Metta Spencer (736 Bathurst, Toronto, ON M5S 2R4 CANADA; office@peacemagazine.org; www.peacemagazine.org)

Reconciliation International, from the International Fellowship of Reconciliation (Spoorstr. 38, 1815 BK Alkmaar, THE NETHERLANDS, office@ifor.org, www.ifor.org)

Resurgence, a journal of alternatives, influenced by E. F. Schumacher and Gandhi, focused mostly on ecology (Subscriptions: Rocksea Farmhouse, St. Mabyn, Bodmin, Cornwall PL30 3BR ENGLAND; Editorial: ed@resurge.demon.co.uk; www.resurgence.org)

Utne Reader, an alternative press (Box 7460, Red Oak IA 51591-0460; 800/736-UTNE)

Vigil, the official publication of Sarva Seva Sangh, the main Gandhian organization in India (Bakharabad, Cuttack, Orissa 753002 INDIA)

BOOKS ON ALTERNATIVE ECONOMICS

(list is from Mark Shepherd, www.markshep.com)

Small is beautiful: Economics as if people mattered, E. F. Schumacher, Harper and Row, 1973. The extremely influential book of an economist most influenced by Gandhi.

Resources/References for Ethical Motivation

The case against the global economy, edited by Jerry Mander and Edward Goldsmith, Sierra Club, 1997. Forty-three essays on the growth of the global economy and its economic, agricultural, cultural, and environmental effects. Selections from such respected writers as Ralph Nader, Richard Barnet, Wendell Berry, and Jeremy Rifkin.

Human scale, Kirkpatrick Sale, Putnam, 1982. The most comprehensive collection of historical and contemporary information ever assembled in support of small-scale economics and government.

Food first: Beyond the myth of scarcity, by Frances Moore Lappé, Ballantine, 1979. How world hunger is created not by poor farming conditions but by land monopoly, large-scale agriculture, and export economies.

Gandhi today: The story of Mahatma Gandhi's successors, Mark Shepard, Simple Productions, Seven Locks Press, 1987 (reprinted from Simple Productions, 1987). My account of a visit with today's Gandhians in India. Focuses in part on their massive efforts for land reform and village development.

The community of the ark, Mark Shepard, Simple Productions, 1990. The account of my visit to a Gandhian community in France, with its dedication to economic self-reliance and simple technology.

Taking charge of our lives: Living responsibly in a troubled world, by the American Friends Service Committee (San Francisco), edited by Joan Bodner, Harper & Row, 1984 (revised edition). Simple living as a political strategy as well as a personal lifestyle. Taking back control from large-scale corporations and returning it to individuals and communities. In the late 1970s, I worked with some of the authors of this book and led workshops on an earlier edition.

The Community land trust handbook, Institute for Community Economics, Rodale Press, 1982. The community land trust was developed as an American version of the Gandhians' Land-Gift and Village-Gift movements in India. Among other things, it has been responsible for significant successes in land preservation.

The Spinner's workshop: A social history and a practical guide, by John Mercer, Prism Press, 1978. Shows how Gandhi's economic ideas applied to Britain's own industrial revolution.

Resources/References for Ethical Motivation

PERIODICALS FOR PEACE

(from Educating for Peace, http://www.global-ed.org/e4p/links.htm)

"Educating for Peace works with the school system to help build a peaceful, just and sustainable world for our children. We believe all teachers can be peace educators. E4P began in 1983 during the Cold War. We see the challenges of that period as still vitally important for students today: to learn to think critically, respect diversity, understand global, cultural and ecological interdependence, analyse the media, examine the nature of violence and learn ways for us all to live more peacefully. To this end we have compiled for teachers and students this latest edition of our Resource Guide for Schools, a collection of classroom-tested materials that will, we believe, help "save succeeding generations from the scourge of war". (United Nations Charter)"

Green Teacher, 5 issues per year. $27 from 95 Robert St. Toronto M5S 2K5, tel.416-960-1244, fax: 416 925-3474. Green teacher is a networking centre for education in ecological concerns, energy studies, alternative technology, and peace and development education. It provides directly usable materials.

Adbusters, 4 issues per year. $18 + GST individuals, $36 + GST institutions, from The Media
Foundation 1243 West 7th Ave., Vancouver, BC V6H 1B7, (604) 736-9401, fax: (604) 737-6021.
Adbusters calls for a media revolution and provides vivid examples of TV propaganda and what we can do about it. Over 400 high schools in North America have subscriptions. Articles on politics and practices of the media and some classroom lesson ideas for use in media literacy courses

Teaching Tolerance from 400 Washington Ave., Montgomery, AL 36104, fax: (334)264-3121
A project of the Southern Poverty Law Center, Teaching Tolerance is a semi-annual magazine offering teachers ready-to-use ideas and strategies for teaching tolerance. Free to teachers with request on school letterhead.

Peace Magazine, 6 issues per year. $17.50 from 736 Bathurst St., Toronto, M5S 2R4, (416)533-7581, fax: (416)531-6214. Canada's national magazine for peace is a leading voice for non-violence. Excellent in-depth articles.

Press for Conversion, 4 times per year. $20 from Coalition to Oppose the Arms Trade (COAT), 541 McLeod St., Ottawa ON K1R 5R2, (613)231-3076, fax: (613)231-2614. Canada's only magazine devoted to the economic conversion of military industries and bases to socially useful and environmentally sound purposes.

Resources/References for Ethical Motivation

Ploughshares, Monitor 4 times per year from Project Ploughshares, Conrad Grebel College, Waterloo, ON N2L 3G6, (519)888-6541. Excellent research and articles in support of disarmament and peace.

Speaking about Rights, newsletter of the Canadian Human Rights Foundation / Paroles de Droits, Bulletin de la fondation canadienne des droits de la personne. From Canadian Human Rights Foundation, 1425 René Lévesque Blvd West, #307 Montréal PQ, H3G 1T7; tel: 514-954-0382; fax: 514- 954-0659; www.chrf.ca).
See especially: "The Culture of Peace" issue, VolXIV No.3 / 1999.

Orbit, magazine of Ontario Institute for Studies in Education, University of Toronto. From 252 Bloor St West Toronto ON M5S 1V6. Tel 416 923-6641
See especially:
Auty, S. (Ed.). (1999). Safe schools. *Orbit, 29*(4).

Bickmore, K. (Ed.). (1997). Teaching conflict resolution: Preparation for pluralism. *Theory into Practice, 36*(1).

Lederach, J. P. (1991). *Beyond prescription: New lenses for conflict resolution training across cultures*. Waterloo, ON: Inter-Racial and Cross-Cultural Conflict Resolution Project.

References for Ethical Motivation

Altman, N. (1980). *Ahimsa.* Wheaton, IL : Theosophical Publishing House.

Ansbro, J. (2000). *Martin Luther King, Jr.: Non-violent strategies and tactics for social change.* Lanham, MD: Madison Books.

Aronson, E., & Patnoe, S. (1997). *The jigsaw classroom: Building cooperation in the classroom.* New York: Longman.

Bennett, W. (1995). *The moral compass.* New York: Simon & Schuster.

Bridgeman, D. (1981). Enhanced role-taking through cooperative interdependence: A field study. *Child Development, 52,* 1231-1238.

Campolo, A., & Aeschliman, G. (1992). *50 ways you can help save the planet.* Downer's Grove, IL: InterVarsity Press.

Carter, S. (1998). *Civility: Manners, morals, and the etiquette of democracy.* New York: Basic Books.

Center for Learning. (1994). *Conflict: A struggle to survive.* Villa Maria, PA: Author.

Center for Learning. (1997). *Hunger: A world view.* Villa Maria, PA: Author.

Collins, A., Hawkins, J., & Carver, S. M. (1991). A cognitive apprenticeship for disadvantaged students. In B. Means, C. Chelemer, & M. S. Knapp (Eds.), *Teaching advanced skills to at-risk students* (pp. 216-243). San Francisco: Jossey Bass.

Crane, S. (1982). *The red badge of courage.* New York: Norton. (Original work published 1895)

Dominguez, J., & Robin, V. (1992). *Your money or your life: transforming your relationship with money and achieving financial independence.* New York: Viking.

Dotson, A., & Dotson, K. (1997). *Teaching character: Teacher's idea book.* Chapel Hill, NC: Character Development Group.

Elgin, D. (1993). *Voluntary simplicity: Toward a way of life that is outwardly simple, inwardly rich.* New York: Quill.

Forni, P. (2002). *Choosing civility: The twenty-five rules of considerate conduct.* New York: St. Martins Press.

Gibbs, J., Potter, G., & Goldstein, A. (1995). *The EQUIP program: Teaching youth to think and act responsibly through a peer-helping approach.* Champaign, IL: Research Press.

Halberstam, J. (1993). *Everyday ethics.* London: Penguin.

Heath, D. (1994). *Schools of hope: Developing mind and character in today's youth.* San Francisco: Jossey-Bass.

Heath, S., & Mangiola, L. (1991). *Children of promise: Literate activity in linguistically and culturally diverse classrooms.* Washington, DC: National Education Association.

Johnson, D. W., & Johnson, F. (1997). *Joining together: Group theory and group skills* (6th ed.). Boston: Allyn & Bacon.

Kekes, J. (1990). *Facing evil.* Princeton, NJ: Princeton University Press.

Kersey, C. (1998). *Unstoppable: 45 powerful stories of perseverance and triumph from people just like you.* Naperville, IL: Sourcebooks.

L'Engle, M. (1962). *A wrinkle in time.* New York: Farrar, Straus, and Giroux.

Lewis, B. A., Espeland, P., & Pernu, C. (1998). *The kid's guide to social action: How to solve the social problems you choose and turn creative thinking into positive action.* Minneapolis, MN: Freespirit.

Lickona, T. (1992). *Educating for character: How our schools can teach respect and responsibility.* New York: Bantam Books, Inc.

Martin, J. (2005). *Miss manners guide to excruciatingly correct behavior.* New York: W.W. Norton.

Maslow, A. (1943). A theory of human motivation. *Psychological Review, 50*(4), 370-396.

Oliner, S. P., & Oliner, P. M. (1988). *The altruistic personality: Rescuers of Jews in Nazi Europe.* New York: The Free Press.

Obsatz, M. (2000). *Healing our anger: Seven ways to make peace in a hostile world.* Minneapolis, MN: Augsburg Fortress Press.

Paul, R. (1987). *Critical thinking handbook, 4th-6th grades: A guide for remodeling lesson plans in language arts, social studies, and science.* Rohnert Park, CA: Center for Critical Thinking and Moral Critique.

Pratkanis, A., & Aronson, E. (1992). *Age of propaganda: The everyday use and abuse of persuasion.* New York: W.H. Freeman.

Pritchard, M. (1996). *Reasonable children.* Lawrence: University of Kansas.

Ross, W. (1930). *The right and the good.* Oxford: Clarendon Press.

Walvoord, B., & Anderson, V. (1998). *Effective grading: A tool for learning and assessment.* San Francisco: Jossey-Bass.

Zukav, G. (1989). *The seat of the soul.* New York: Simon and Schuster.

About the Authors

Darcia Narvaez, Ph.D., Associate Professor of Psychology at the University of Notre Dame, developed the Integrative Ethical Education model (initiated under the federally-funded Minnesota Community Voices and Character Education Project which she reported on at a Whitehouse conference). Previously at the University of Minnesota, she was executive director of the Center for the Study of Ethical Development and was director of the Center for Ethical Education at the University of Notre Dame. She is on the editorial boards of the *Journal of Educational Psychology* and the Journal of Moral Education. She has published in the *Journal of Educational Psychology, Developmental Psychology,* and has two award-winning books, *Postconventional Moral Thinking* (1999; with Rest, Bebeau & Thoma) and *Moral Development, Self and Identity* (2004; with Lapsley).

James Lies, C.S.C., Ph.D., is Assistant Professor of Psychology in the Department of Social and Behavioral Sciences at the University of Portland, and a priest of the Congregation of Holy Cross. Having received his Ph.D. in educational psychology from the University of Minnesota in 2005, he completed a post-doctoral appointment at the Center on Adolescence at Stanford University in 2006. His research has examined the effects of service-learning on the moral reasoning of late adolescents, and looked at moral identity, moral reasoning, and religiosity as possible predictors of service. While at the University of Minnesota, he was involved in the Community Voices and Character Education Project, the character education program for public middle schools from which this EthEx Series has been developed. Prior to attaining his Ph.D., he had previously received an M.A. in counseling from the University of Notre Dame and a Master of Divinity degree from the Graduate Theological Union at Berkeley.

www.ingramcontent.com/pod-product-compliance
Lightning Source LLC
Chambersburg PA
CBHW081148090426
42736CB00017B/3235

* 9 7 8 0 9 8 1 9 5 0 1 2 9 *